CONTEMPORARY AFRICA

CONTINENT IN TRANSITION

T. WALTER WALLBANK

Professor of History
University of Southern California

AN ANVIL ORIGINAL

under the general editorship of

LOUIS L. SNYDER

D. VAN NOSTRAND COMPANY, INC.

PRINCETON, NEW JERSEY

TORONTO   LONDON

NEW YORK

To

JOAN AND TOM

and our happy days in Africa

D. VAN NOSTRAND COMPANY, INC.

120 Alexander St., Princeton, New Jersey
257 Fourth Avenue, New York 10, New York
25 Hollinger Rd., Toronto 16, Canada
Macmillan & Co., Ltd., St. Martin's St.,
London, W.C. 2, England

*All correspondence should be addressed to the
principal office of the company at Princeton, N. J.*

PREFACE

Only a few decades ago Africa was taken for granted and complacently ignored. It was regarded as a static and unimportant Dark Continent populated by backward tribes with queer customs. For many, knowledge of Africa was restricted to the writings of Rider Haggard, Frank Buck, Trader Horn, and Martin Johnson. This period of complacency is symbolized for the author by his membership in a seminar at the London School of Economics. Another member, seemingly quite moderate in his views, was Jomo Kenyatta, a young Kikuyu from Kenya Colony. There seemed to be little discontent, little dynamism in Africa at that time. But those static days have disappeared. The young Kikuyu African, as a case in point, returned to Kenya via Moscow to become one of the organizers of the ruthless, anti-European society of the Mau Mau.

It has taken little more than a decade to launch Africa into the full stream of world affairs. Today its economic and strategic importance looms large, not only to the colonial powers of western Europe but also to the United States. Africa is a land where people are on the march, imbued with new faiths, especially nationalism, and armed with confidence in their destiny. This small volume has only the modest aim of presenting the salient facts, the fundamental trends, in the African story, with special reference to the significant developments of the past fifteen years. North Africa, because it is Arabic in culture and long oriented to Europe and the Middle East, is not included in this survey. The subject of this volume is the real Africa, that part of the huge continent populated by the Bantu and Negro peoples south of the Sahara.

In the writing of this book the author expresses his appreciation for the assistance rendered by various Embassies and Information Services, both in the United States and in Africa: those of Great Britain, France,

Belgium, Portugal, South Africa, the Gold Coast, the Federation of Rhodesia and Nyasaland, and the South African Institute of Race Relations. Lastly, a word of gratitude to the Social Science Research Council, which in 1937 gave me my first opportunity to visit Africa and study its problems.

Julian, California   T. WALTER WALLBANK

TABLE OF CONTENTS

Part I

CONTEMPORARY AFRICA
Continent in Transition

— 1 —

AFRICA AND TODAY'S WORLD

Africa in Ferment. Rapid change, tension, and unrest are now characteristic of what was only recently the unchanging Dark Continent. Since World War II, a scant decade ago, African nationalism has grown at breakneck speed. The first prime minister of a self-governing Negro nation, formerly a British colony, has appeared to head the government of the Gold Coast. In the Union of South Africa there have been serious clashes between the Whites and the Blacks and continuous discord and turmoil. In British Central Africa, after much controversy, a major political development has taken place as European settlers have united to form the Federation of Rhodesia and Nyasaland. In British Kenya the long-smoldering discontents of the largest native tribe have broken out in the terrible brutalities of the Mau Mau.

This study will be concerned with only sub-Saharan Africa, the home of the Negro. Mediterranean Africa, now predominantly Moslem in culture, is to be sure suffused with nationalism and discontent, but this area has always been oriented to Europe and the Middle East and hence lies out of our sphere of interest. And as most of the challenging problems and dynamic trends, together with the bulk of the population, are found in British territories, this volume will place major emphasis upon British Africa.

Some Basic Problems. Africa on the surface today is a fascinating and complex pattern of mixed and criss-crossing forces. For simplicity's sake then these can be grouped into four basic types of problems.

(1) Africa is the last great home of empire. Rapid liquidation of colonial rule is taking place, but with much less experience and training in self-government than in former colonial dependencies like India or the Philippines. What of the future? Will these newly emancipated peoples be able to develop efficient, progressive, and stable regimes?

(2) Africa also poses the acute problem of the *plural society,* which was defined by the scholar who invented this term as "a society comprising two or more elements or social orders which live side by side, yet without mingling, in one political unit." [1] In East, Central, and South Africa people of different color must contrive ways and means to enable Europeans, Africans, and East Indians to live cooperatively and harmoniously in the same society. Africa is par excellence a laboratory for one of the contemporary world's greatest problems, that of race relations.

(3) In common with much of the Middle East and Asia, Africa presents the dangers and the sufferings inherent in a continent whose resources are both underdeveloped and wastefully used. Agriculture must be modernized to support rising populations. Government revenues must be increased to expand educational and public-health facilities, for without literate, healthy, and economically progressive populations, the self-governing African nations of the near future will be doomed to failure before they even achieve their independence.

(4) Coloring and conditioning all three previous problems is the impact of Western culture upon the traditional life of Africa. Everywhere the Negro feels the unsettling effect of European ways and manners as he works in mines, toils on plantations, or busies himself as a houseboy in a white family's home. The new gospel of the Christian missionary and the edicts and taxes of the European official also are part of a strange world in which increasingly he finds himself. His tribal loyalties, ancient gods, and family customs are either being swept away or drastically weakened by the impact of the new culture.

Is the African destined eventually to surrender entirely his ancient ways for those of the white man? Can

[1] J. S. Furnivall, *Netherlands India* (Cambridge University Press, 1939) p. 446.

he somehow work for and mingle with Europeans and yet retain his distinctive way of life as is proposed in the *apartheid* policy of the Union of South Africa? Or is the African fated to lose the old culture that once gave meaning and direction to his life, without being able to assimilate the alien culture of the West? If this last be true, the African would become a man between two worlds, no longer of the old but unable to be part of the new.

Some Basic Facts. Africa is the second largest of the continents, more than 11,530,000 square miles in extent, exceeding by three times the size of Europe. North to south from Bizerte to the Cape of Good Hope it extends 5000 miles; and east to west from Dakar to Cape Guardafui the distance is 4600 miles. Though census figures are still unreliable, the population south of the Sahara is in the neighborhood of 120 million. Outside the 12 million inhabitants of the independent state of the Union of South Africa, the vast majority of people in sub-Saharan Africa live in one of four great colonial systems: The British (57 million), the French (29 million), the Belgian (11 million), and the Portuguese (9½ million). Of these, only 3 million are western Europeans, plus 750,000 East Indians and a sprinkling of Arabs, Greeks, Syrians, and other peoples. Two thirds of the Europeans and half of the Indians live in South Africa. Outside South Africa the greatest concentrations of non-Africans are found in French West Africa, British Kenya, and the Belgian Congo.

Sub-Saharan Africa is a land of unusual diversity, combining scenic features of great beauty and harsh ugliness. Here astride the equator are some of the world's greatest mountains, perpetually mantled with snow. Vast deserts give way to rolling steppe lands, hot and muggy coastal plains, or dense and impenetrable jungle areas. One of the features of sub-Saharan Africa is its great plateau. If a line be drawn from Benguela on the lower west coast through Stanleyville on the upper Congo River to Suakin on the Red Sea, to the south and east is a great highland region over 3000 feet in altitude except along the coast. It is in these highlands that European settlement is possible, even on the equator itself. As to resources, Africa can claim to have one quarter of the earth's potential cropland. On the whole, however, the continent south of the Sahara has poor and deep soil and suffers from many impediments to agriculture. It is, on the other hand, unique in its wealth of certain valuable and strategic minerals and has vast resources of water power waiting to be harnessed.

Three Racial Groups. All Africans belong to the Negro race, but it is more correct to divide this into three great groups—the true Negro, the Half-Hamites and Nilotes, and the Bantu. These, in turn, break down into hundreds of different peoples and tribes, each with its own distinctive cultural and sometimes physical characteristics. The true Negro is found mainly on the Guinea Coast of West Africa and is identified by his black skin, woolly hair, flat and broad nose, thick lips, and often considerable prognathism. Examples of this racial type are the Mandingo, Ashanti, Yoruba, and Hausa. The true Negro was the race brought to the New World by the slave trade. But there has been considerable mixing of white blood with that of the Negro. Hamitic peoples of the Caucasoid family entered Africa in a series of ethnic invasions, often intermarrying with the indigenous people (or on occasion exterminating them). The result is the Hamiticized Negroes. These are limited to East and east Central Africa and include such tribes as the Masai, Nandi, and Lumbwe. These tall and aristocratic people are great cattle tenders, with skin that is reddish-brown rather than black. A closely related group is found in the Nile Valley south of Khartoum, exemplified by the Dinka and the Shilluk.

The third racial group, and the largest, is the Bantu. These people are the dominant human type in East and South Africa. Occupying one third of the entire continent, the Bantu are basically Negro, with Hamitic characteristics that betray their mixed racial origin. Some of the important tribes in this Bantu race are the Baganda, Kikuyu, Basuto, Matabele, and Zulu.

Africa in World Civilization. Africa is a land with little or no history. South of the Sahara the indigenous peoples cannot look back on any golden age, on any truly great civilization. Of the twenty-one outstanding cultures in world history listed by the English historian Toynbee, none is Negro. It has been truly said that "Africa south of the Sahara has always been poor and powerless. The political and cultural emptiness of the African past is the key to any understanding of the continent's present problems." [2] This generalization holds true despite the efforts of some Negro intellectuals to discover periods of greatness in the African past. The African produced no alphabets, no adequate system of numerals, no calendar or exact measurements, no currency, plough, or wheel. He built few towns and created nothing that could endure. Worst of all, he was a creature of fear and superstition, helpless in the grip of magic and witchcraft.

The backwardness of Africa is, indeed, one of the ironies of history, for on this continent originated and flourished one of the first of civilizations. The real key to African history, however, is the continent's isolation. The great barrier of the Sahara, more than one thousand miles across, has been a veritable iron curtain inhibiting the flow and exchange of culture from north to south. And below the great desert there stretches an impenetrable coast, practically unindented and graced by few good harbors. The rivers, what few of them there are that flow to the sea, discourage navigation with their treacherous rapids and fever-ridden deltas. Furthermore, behind the coastal plain there is often a high plateau whose steep side has effectively discouraged inland penetration.

The Africans' Potentialities. In addition to physical obstacles, nature has handicapped human progress by its menace of pests and microbes. One of the greatest of African explorers observed: "Africa is the chief stronghold of the real Devil—the reactionary forces of Nature hostile to the rise of Humanity. Here Belzebub, King of the Flies, marshals his vermiform and anthropoid hosts—insects, ticks, and nematode worms—which . . . convey to the skin, veins, intestines, and spinal marrow of men and other vertebrates the microorganisms which cause deadly, disfiguring, or debilitating diseases." [3] Perhaps the greatest single enemy of progress in Africa today is the deadly tsetse fly responsible for sleeping sickness.

[2] Cornelis W. de Kiewiet, "African Dilemmas," *Foreign Affairs*, April 1955, p. 448.

[3] Harry H. Johnston, *The Negro in the New World* (London, 1910) pp. 14-15.

Notwithstanding his backwardness and his failure to contribute in the past to world civilization, the African does not belong to an inferior race. Anthropologists and colonial experts speak of his artistic genius and his many admirable qualities, such as amiability and innate cheerfulness. And intelligence tests have not revealed that the Negro is substantially inferior to the European. It is quite true that the African has certain weaknesses. In thinking, emotion tends to dominate and his energy is spasmodic. It is hard for an African to work toward a distant goal. But these weaknesses are characteristic of primitive peoples all over the world. When the deadening effects of black magic, disease, and the retrogressive tyranny of tribal conservatism have been removed, an educated African in motivation, energy, and logical thought processes is no different from the college-trained Englishman or Frenchman. The backwardness of sub-Saharan Africa has been caused by the tyranny of an unfriendly and harsh nature, plus the ageless isolation from the outside world. In Toynbee's terms, there has not been sufficient culture stimulation from other centers and the challenge of nature has been too strong.

Africa in World Affairs.   Since World War II Africa has emerged as a new factor in world affairs. The poverty of western Europe following World War II and the contraction of its economic foundation, resulting from the loss of its colonies in Asia, have caused Europeans to turn to Africa as, at least, a partial solution of their economic problems. Increasing trade with sub-Saharan Africa promises an outlet for European capital and skills, the lessening of difficult currency problems (especially the dollar shortage), access to valuable raw materials, and some possibility of an area for settling surplus population. Europeans, moreover, realize that the post-1945 relationship must forgo any remnants left of the old ruthless imperialism and be squarely based on the new concept of partnership.

Africa is now seen in a new light by Europeans—but also by Americans. Though there has been a long connection between Africa and the United States, it was not a close or vital one until a decade ago. In the early nineteenth century American whalers plied their skill in African waters and traded here and there. Americans also became interested in missionary activity and supported the little Republic of Liberia. During World War II Africa assumed vital importance to America's war effort as its ports, such as Freetown, Cape Town, Lourenço Marques, and Mombasa, were crowded with merchant vessels carrying troops and supplies to the all-important war theater in the Middle East. New airfields were also constructed to take care of thousands of planes shuttling back and forth from east to west. The rising importance of Africa was recognized by the American State Department when it created a Division of African Affairs with the Office of Eastern and African Affairs.

Following World War II Africa continued to occupy an important place in American national interest. With the unhappy advent of the cold war it was apparent that African resources and strategic position were extremely important for the defense of the free world. Should communication lines in the Mediterranean be blocked, men and supplies could be sent by air across Africa or around the continent by water into the Indian Ocean. Africa has also become one of the most important producers of valuable raw materials, indispensable to the defense effort of the United States. The following figures illustrate this point. We import from Africa 97% of our columbium ore, 81% of our palm oil, 68% of our cobalt, 52% of our industrial diamonds, and 23% of our manganese ore. As to uranium, statistics are not available, but we know that our largest single source of this element is the Belgian Congo.

In addition to our traditional support of such humanitarian work as missionary, educational, and medical enterprise, the United States is concerned with Africa for reasons of national interest. It is essential that this rising continent remain friendly to the West and that its indispensable raw materials and strategic areas continue to be available. At present a great tide of nationalism, an urge to be free, is agitating masses of Africans south of the Sahara. Traditionally we favor this aspiration toward self-determination. At the same time, however, it is apparent that the pace of emancipation may be too swift. In our present complex world if people are unprepared for the responsibilities of nationhood, their governments will likely be unstable and inefficient. And this condition invites aggression and impedes economic progress.

Confronted with this great continent now in transition, the role of the United States is a difficult one. We cannot obstruct fundamental forces of history, such as modern nationalism, but it may be possible to influence the tempo of their pace and to do something to build a favorable atmosphere for their being. America can do much with economic and technical aid to prepare Africans for their eventual goal of national freedom, and at the same time we should support and encourage all efforts of the colonial powers in Africa to prepare their colonial peoples for self-government. But equally important, we must be sympathetic with the imperial powers as they seek solutions to the many problems inherent in this great transition from colonialism to "nationism."

— 2 —

EXPLORATION, PARTITION, COLONIZATION

Africa in Ancient Times. The great span of history as far as Africa south of the Sahara is concerned, up to little more than a century ago is shrouded in mystery. We know that the ancient Egyptians made voyages down the east coast and also ventured far up the Nile, the most famous expedition being that sent by Queen Hatshepusut about 1470 B.C., which might have reached Cape Guardafui. Next, about 600 B.C. according to the Greek historian Herodotus, the Pharaoh Necho sent some Phoenician mariners to sail around Africa which they supposedly did in three years. About this time the Phoenician traders were very active along the west coast. Then comes one of the greatest recorded explorations of ancient times. This was the expedition led by Hanno, organized by Carthage, consisting of sixty ships. Leaving the Mediterranean in 520 B.C., this great fleet rounded Cape Verde on the west coast and reached Sierra Leone. As a result of this and other voyages the Carthaginians maintained trading posts along the Atlantic coast of North Africa as far south as the inlet now called Rio de Oro.

Coming to Greek and Roman times, Herodotus in the sixth century B.C. is reported to have explored parts of Egypt and to have heard about a great river called the Niger. The Romans, neglecting the west coast of Africa, concentrated on trade with Arabia, East Africa, and India. About 40 A.D., the secret of the monsoon was discovered, and Roman vessels could get to India more quickly and venture down the African east coast. In the second century A.D. the famous astronomer and geographer of Alexandria, Ptolemy, had apparently learned of the junction of the two Nile Rivers, the Blue and the White. He believed that the source of the Blue Nile was in a great lake to the east and that the origin of the White Nile was in African lakes fed from the Mountains of the Moon. These suppositions were proved to be true by modern explorers. To one looking back, it is apparent that there was little contact between sub-Saharan Africa and the Greco-Roman world. It has been pointed out that not a single artifact identified with tropical Africa has also been identified as belonging to the period of the Greeks and Romans.

Moslems in the Sudan. In early medieval times important contacts in Africa were made by Moslems. This penetration began with the conquest of Egypt in 640 A.D. by the followers of Mohammed. By 711 the men of Allah had swept across the entire North African coast. These Moslems spread southwards into the Sudan in the regions of Lake Chad, Darfur, Kordofan, and Kano. Stopping short of the coast because of the barrier of forest and the deadly tsetse fly, these invaders—many of them Islamized Berber tribes—settled down in the fertile valleys of the Niger and the Senegal.

The result was the creation of a great Arabic-Berber civilization in western Sudan. From 1200 to 1500 this area had close contact with North Africa and Moslem Spain, sharing their art, literature, and science. A number of great Afro-Moslem kingdoms flourished, such as

Songhay, Ghana, Melle, and Bornu. In many respects
these states, in degree of civilization, were the equal to
the most advanced in western Europe. The kingdom of
Songhay stretched 1500 miles east to west. And in this
great area the rule of law and a common administrative
system were given to many diverse subjects. Its capital,
Timbuktu, was justly famous as a great trading center
where hundreds of great caravans converged, some with
as many as 12,000 camels. Here at Timbuktu was a great
mosque and attached to it a famous school or university
of Koranic studies. Songhay boasted a fine architecture
patterned after Egyptian and Saracenic models. Its breeds
of horses were unexcelled, its iron, tin, and leather goods
eagerly sought. In the fifteenth century, Songhay and
other Afro-Moslem states rapidly declined. West Africa
was deprived of its former stimulating Moslem contacts
with Spain and the Mediterranean. Disorder and wars
followed, and the Sudan subsided into decadence.

Zenj Empire and Zimbabwe. Moslems were also
active along the African east coast. From ancient times
seamen from Oman, the states of the Persian Gulf, and
the northwest coast of India had been sailing to East
Africa in their dhows. The first settlement took place on
the coast in the late seventh century and was followed
by many others from Arabia and Persia. From 975 to
1497—before the coming of the Portuguese—the whole
of the coast was controlled by a number of states, such
as Mombasa, Kilwa, Lamu, under the supremacy of the
sultanate of Kilwa. These little states composed collec-
tively what is known as the Zenj Empire and the coast
known as Zenjibar (which means *black coast*). A profit-
able trade was carried on in slaves, ivory, and gold. The
most important source of the gold was at Sofala, a port
located in the present Portuguese colony of Mozambique.
Sofala seems to have been the export center for the rich
gold mines of the African hinterland, mainly what is now
Southern Rhodesia. In this area between the Limpopo and
Zambezi rivers many ancient monuments and remains
have been discovered, especially those at Zimbabwe. Who
built these magnificent fortresses is still a moot point:
Was it the Phoenicians, the Arabs, or some highly en-
dowed African nation now extinct?

The Coming of the Portuguese. European contact

with sub-Saharan Africa began in the fifteenth century. It never ceased, becoming stronger and more decisive with each passing century until, after five hundred years, all of the Africa we are concerned with had passed under the control of Europeans. Little Portugal initiated what we know as the expansion of Europe; its early history constitutes the first chapters in the story of the creation of modern colonial empires. The first act in this drama was the capture by the Portuguese of the Moslem stronghold of Ceuta on the African coast opposite Gibraltar. One of the outstanding warriors and leaders in medieval Europe now took charge. Combining the zeal of a crusader, the curiosity of a scientist, and the hope for gain of a merchant, Prince Henry (1394-1460), son of the Portuguese king, determined to explore Africa. Especially was his heart set on sending his little ships down into the mysterious and unknown coastal waters of West Africa. Legend had it that these were seas of terror, full of monsters, boiling water, and pestilential air.

Such hazards did not deter Prince Henry. By 1434 Cape Bojador was passed and by 1445 Cape Verde had been rounded. A few years later, tangible proof of the value of these voyages was brought to Lisbon when African slaves and gold were exhibited in the capital. In 1471, eleven years after Henry's death, the equator was crossed by Portuguese mariners; in 1482 the mouth of the Congo was reached. Then came the voyage of Bartholomeu Dias in 1486 by which he reached the Cape of Good Hope, the southern tip of the continent; and in 1497 the voyage of Vasco da Gama rounding the Cape and sailing up the east coast, thence eastward to India.

Portugal had thus broken the Arab's monopoly of the rich spice and luxury trade of the Far East. Forts and trading posts were set up around Africa and Arabia to protect Portuguese shipping. The first permanent European settlement was set up on the Gold Coast in 1482 by the Portuguese, with their castle at Elmina. Other posts were established near Dakar and on various rivers such as the Gambia and the Congo; and after 1597 a colony was firmly built in Angola. For some seventy-five years the Portuguese monopoly in Africa went unchallenged, but early in the seventeenth century it was challenged and virtually destroyed by the Dutch. Portugal,

with its scant two million people was not strong enough
to develop and defend its vast colonial holdings. Despite
its responsibility for embarking on the traffic in slaves,
Portugal contributed materially in the long run to the
welfare of the African people. Important plants were
brought to Africa from Brazil, such as pineapples, sweet
potatoes, peanuts, sweet corn, oranges, and limes. Various
breeds of cattle, fowls, many utensils, and weapons were
also introduced.

Slavery and Trade Rivalries.   English trade activity
on the African west coast began in the 1550's, the first
important voyage being made to the Gulf of Guinea in
1553. The redoubtable Elizabethan sea dog, John Hawk-
ins, made the first of three voyages in 1562 and initiated
the English slave trade resulting in the first African slaves
being taken to the colony of Virginia in 1620. As West
Africa became a reservoir of labor for the American
colonies, the traders of many nations came in their ships
and set up their forts on the Guinea coast. There were
English, French, Dutch, Danes, Swedes, and others. Having supplanted the Portuguese, the Dutch in turn were
challenged by the French and especially the English, who
had built their first permanent settlement of Fort James
on the Gambia. As to the French, their traders made
their first important voyage to Senegal in 1637 and built
the strategic post of St.-Louis in 1658.

From the time of the collapse of Portugal's dominant
position in the last quarter of the sixteenth century to the
end of the eighteenth, West Africa was continually con-
vulsed by the rivalries and the incessant fighting of the
trading nations. The British finally emerged as the masters
of the Gold Coast area over the Dutch. On the coast
between the Gambia and the Senegal the French in the
closing years of the eighteenth century lost all their settlements to their rivals, the English. Following the end
of the Napoleonic Wars, however, Britain returned these
captured posts to France who, as we will see shortly, proceeded to use them as the foundations for a great West
African Empire.

Despite their failure on the west coast, the Dutch made
a notable contribution in South Africa. When their ships
first began the long voyage around Africa to the East
Indian Islands, they stopped at the island of St. Helena

for supplies. The Dutch East India Company then directed one of its officials to proceed to South Africa, where in 1652 a landing was made at Table Bay, the site of the modern Cape Town. Here the leader, Jan van Riebeeck, established a supply base where fresh fruits and vegetables could be obtained to combat the ever-present menace of scurvy. This Tavern of the Seas was also used to mail letters. Ships sailing eastward could leave letters to be picked up by those going in the opposite direction, to Holland. It became the custom to leave these letters under the so-called Post-Office Stones. From a revictualing station the Cape Settlement gradually grew into a colony. Settlers came from Holland, and in 1689 a number of Huguenots landed from France.

The Dutch found two native stocks in South Africa: the primitive Bushmen and the Hottentots. The former were driven into the interior. Even before the advent of Europeans the Bushmen were declining rapidly in numbers. Today only a few pathetic remnants are left. The Hottentots, a pastoral people, tried to resist the Dutch advance but soon succumbed and became the servants of the invaders. As the demand for labor mounted, however, the Dutch imported substantial numbers of slaves from Madagascar and the East African coast. In the century that followed, Hottentots, slaves, and some European stock mingled to form the people now known as the "Cape Colored."

As the Cape Settlement grew, the hardier burghers pushed inland, crossing rivers and mountains to reach the interior high plateau or veld. At the same time from the north came well-organized and warlike Bantu tribes such as the Zulu and Matabele. These two streams of migration met in the valley of the Fish River, and all along the line of contact sporadic raiding and fighting took place. Between 1779 and 1877 there were nine major Kaffir wars. These Dutch frontier farmers, known as Boers, called all Bantus "Kaffirs," a term derived from the Arabic word meaning *infidel*. In addition to the advent of the Bantu, the close of the eighteenth century witnessed the coming of the Briton. During the struggle with Napoleon a British fleet anchored in Table Bay in 1795, and a garrison occupied Cape Town until 1802. After leaving for four years, the British returned in 1806 to stay on after the defeat of the Little Corporal, for Cape Colony was formally ceded to Britain in 1814 by the Treaty of Paris.

While these various European settlements were being made, their traders were carrying on a nefarious traffic in black ivory. The slave trade was not originated by Europeans, but they expanded and systematized it. Slavery was common in ancient Egypt, which continually raided the Sudan for its man power. It was also carried on by the Romans, the Byzantines, and the Arabs. It was, however, European merchants who, spurred on by the enormous profits, brought the slave trade to the enormous proportions that it reached in the eighteenth century. English merchants, especially from Liverpool, led those of all other nations. It has been estimated that between 1680 and 1786 their ships carried a total of 2,000,000 slaves. In the closing years of the eighteenth century the annual figures ran about 100,000 slaves; and for the first fifty years in the next century the annual figure was not much less than 85,000. The trade based on this human misery was a triangular one. Guns, gin, trinkets, and cloth left Europe for West Africa to pay for the slaves. These then were transported to the Americas in exchange for furs, sugar, molasses, ships' stores, hardwoods, and the like. These products were then delivered to the markets of Europe at a handsome profit.

The cruelties of "the middle passage" surpass belief. The great eighteenth-century reformer, William Wilberforce, declared: "Never can so much misery be found condensed into so small a space as in a slave-ship." It is said that for every 300 slaves alive in the Americas after one year, 700 had died. During the raids in Africa and during the harrowing march to the coast, 500 perished. In the packed holds of the slave ships another 125 died; and finally, another 75 died after landing in the New World!

Emancipation and Exploration.   If England was the leader in this enterprise of horror, it is to her credit that Englishmen were the first to take up cudgels against it. Part and parcel of the strong humanitarian movement, the fight against slavery was initiated by Granville Sharp. This reformer's work was carried on by William Clarkson and William Wilberforce, who organized in 1787 the

Committee for the Abolition of the Slave Trade. This same year the committee transported 351 liberated slaves from England to the coast of Sierra Leone. In 1788 another expedition was sent out, and four years later more than one thousand Negroes were settled at the new center of Freetown. Meanwhile in the British Parliament Wilberforce and his friends introduced bill after bill to abolish the slave trade. In 1807 victory was achieved. In the same year President Jefferson approved a bill imposing heavy penalties on anyone bringing slaves into the United States. In 1817 France followed suit, and in 1833 the Abolition of Slavery Bill was passed by Parliament, ending slavery throughout the British Empire. Other nations —France in 1848 and Holland in 1863—followed this lead. The task of hunting down the slave ships was mainly the responsibility of the Royal Navy, whose West African squadron, based on Freetown, was in continuous action for fifty years. The slave trade on the East African coast persisted after that on the west coast had been virtually stomped out. The Arab dhows, carrying slaves to the Middle East, were difficult to intercept. By 1860, however, the end of the slave trade in this area was in sight; and in 1863 a telling blow against slavery itself was struck by President Lincoln's Emancipation Proclamation.

The systematic exploration of Africa may be dated from the formation of the African Association in 1788. Formed by the enthusiasm of the noted scientist, Sir Joseph Banks, this body was formed "to promote the cause of science and humanity, to explore the mysterious geography, to ascertain the resources, and to improve the condition of that ill-fated continent." As the eighteenth century closed, practically nothing was known about the interior of Africa by the outside world. A trading station here and there on the coast and a settlement of Boers and British in Cape Colony were Europe's only impress on the Dark Continent. In the space of about seventy-five years, however, a number of intrepid explorers traced the course of the main rivers, crossed the deadly Sahara from North Africa to the Sudan, revealed the majesty of Lake Victoria, and traversed the almost impenetrable jungle land from the west coast on the Atlantic to the East African coast on the Indian Ocean.

The English African Association sent out the famous explorer, Mungo Park, in 1795 and again in 1804 to trace the course of the Niger River. On both occasions this river was reached, but before Park was able to trace its course he was murdered by unfriendly natives in 1805. Meanwhile another English party, composed of Oudney, Clapperton, and Denham left Tripoli and in 1821-1822 crossed the Sahara, reaching Lake Chad in central Sudan. At the same time a resourceful French explorer, René Caillié, had traveled through Senegambia to the legendary city of Timbuktu, then turned north, crossing the desert to Morocco. Caillié was the first European to reach Timbuktu and return. The vexing problem of the Niger was finally solved by Richard Lander and his brother. Acting for the British Government, they traced the great stream to the coast in 1830, proving that the so-called Oil Rivers were the delta of the Niger. This West African exploration reached a climax in the early 1850's with the work of Dr. Heinrich Barth. This German was perhaps the most remarkable of all explorers in this area. He visited the most important cities of western Sudan and with Teutonic thoroughness studied the geography, history, and ethnology of the country. His volumes on his travels still remain classics in the story of African exploration.

Livingstone and Stanley. The opening up of East and Central Africa will always be associated with the travels of Livingstone, Stanley, Speke, and Grant. The first was sent to South Africa as a medical missionary by the London Missionary Society. Becoming more interested in exploration than in Christianization, Livingstone on his first great journey of discovery found Victoria Falls and crossed Africa, east to west (1852 to 1856). It was on this journey that he came into contact with the horrors of East African slavery, which he called "the open sore of the world." Returning to England after the greatest feat in African exploration, Livingstone gave his historic address at the University of Cambridge which stimulated interest in Africa throughout the Western world. After a second journey, which led him to Lake Nyasa (1858-1864), Livingstone began his third and last (1856-1873). Disappearing into the African bush, "the Good Doctor" was able to send no word to the outside world for five years. Finally, the New York *Herald* sent H. M. Stanley, a famous foreign correspondent, to find Livingstone—and make one of the great news scoops of the day. (*See Reading No. 1.*) Refusing to come home with Stanley, Livingstone, though weak and old before his time, continued with his explorations. The rigors of the jungle, however, were too much and on May 1, 1873, his faithful followers found him dead in a praying position beside his cot. His body was carried hundreds of miles to the coast by his servants and finally was laid to rest in Westminster Abbey, where his memory remains "a model to explorers and an inspiration to Mankind."

While Livingstone was just concluding his first great journey, two Englishmen in 1856 had been sent by the Royal Geographical Society to check on the existence of a great inland lake in the interior of East Africa. John Speke had already made a name for himself exploring the Himalayas and Tibet, and Richard Burton was a romantic figure who had amazed the world by traveling to and entering the sacred city of Mecca. Starting on their thousand-mile journey from the African east coast, these two discovered Lake Tanganyika. With Burton ill, Speke pushed on another two hundred miles to discover Lake Victoria, a majestic body of water 26,000 square miles in extent. Instead of reporting back to Burton, Speke rushed home to England to publicize his discovery and to claim finding the source of the Nile. A second expedition, headed by Speke and accompanied by J. A. Grant, explored Lake Victoria more thoroughly (1860-1863) and made the first visit of Europeans to Uganda. They also saw the White Nile pouring from Lake Victoria at Ripon Falls and then followed the great river to Khartoum and hence through Egypt to the Mediterranean.

Other explorers who made their mark in the opening of the Dark Continent might be briefly mentioned. James Bruce as early as 1768-1773 journeyed into Egypt and Abyssinia to reveal the source of the Blue Nile. The Frenchman Gaspard Mollien, disguised as a trader, discovered the sources of the Senegal and Gambia rivers (1818); and Count de Brazza, likewise French, from 1874 to 1884 explored scientifically the whole region of Libreville on the Gaboon River and the north banks of

the Congo and Ubangi. The work of German explorers
was also very significant. In the 1860's men like Dr.
Rohlfs and Dr. Schweinfurth explored the Sudan and
Central Africa. In East Africa, Krapf revealed for the
first time the snow-covered peak of Mount Kenya
(1849), and his countryman Rebmann did the same thing
for Mount Kilimanjaro. Dr. Nachtigal also did notable
work in the eastern Sahara. These Germans represented
a new type of explorer. Interested in science rather than
mere geographical discoveries, they collected valuable
data on all aspects of the lands they traversed. Speaking of
Schweinfurth, the late Prime Minister of South Africa,
General Smuts, once said that his *Heart of Africa* was
one of the most interesting and valuable books of African
travel ever written.

Stanley had found the lure of Africa on his first mission and he soon returned to solve some of the problems
left by Livingstone. From 1874 to 1877 he made his
epochal journey of 999 days in which he circled Lake
Victoria, and traveling westward, followed the Congo
down to the sea. It was this expedition that marked the
end of the classic period of African exploration and
introduces the next great historic period—that of the
scramble for territory, sometimes referred to as the Great
African Colony Hunt.

The Great Colony Hunt. By 1870 the interest in
Africa was mounting rapidly. Unostentatiously, France
had been extending her influence throughout West Africa.
In particular in the 1850's the governor of French Senegal, General Faidherbe, laid the foundations for a great
colonial empire. Extending French control far into the
interior, he opened the road to the Niger and central
Sudan. At the same time, during the reign of Louis
Philippe, French trading posts were reactivated along
the Guinea and Ivory Coasts and in Dahomey. While
not especially eager at first, the British also were expanding their influence in Africa. In 1807 Sierra Leone had
definitely become a crown colony, and by 1874, despite
the recent recommendation of a Parliamentary committee to abandon most of the British posts along the west
coast, the Gold Coast had been made a British crown
colony. The same action was also taken along the
Nigerian coast when Lagos was made a colony in 1861.

In South Africa, Britain was becoming involved more and more in problems stemming from the clash of interests between Briton, Boer, and Bantu. And these problems arose not only in Cape Colony but far into the interior.

After 1815 ugly clashes became more frequent between the English authorities and the Boers. The latter were furious over the emancipation of the slaves in 1833 and over making English the official language in 1828. In 1836 the Great Trek began. An epic movement of some five thousand Boers moving in their great waggons hauled by oxen back into the interior to the high veld. There was fierce fighting with the Zulus. A treacherous massacre carried out by the native leader, Dingaan, was later avenged by the Boers when three thousand Zulus were killed and scarcely a Boer hurt. This victory, known as Dingaan's Day even today is celebrated by all Boers. Ejected from what became the British colony of Natal in 1843, the Boers set up two independent states: the South African Republic or the Transvaal, and the Orange River Free State. All through the high veld from the Orange to the Vaal River and beyond there were some ten thousand Boers. These *voortrekkers* developed into a remarkable people. Basing their religion on the Old Testament, they believed implicitly in the superiority of the white over the black; to them God had given divine sanction to be the *baas* (master) over the Kaffirs. The Boers were passionately fond of their freedom, attached to their tongue, Afrikaans, and distrustful of all innovation from the outside. Being fiercely individualistic, the Boers often had their political feuds and at times a number of petty republics were set up. At the same time there was constant trouble with the Bantus. Despite its wishes, Britain found itself involved in these troubles. In 1848 the British governor of the Cape announced the sovereignty of Britain between the Orange and Vaal rivers. After all, these Boers had been British subjects in the Cape. But native wars and other involvements were a heavy drain on the imperial exchequer, and in 1852 the British gave recognition to the independence of the Transvaal, followed two years later by similar action for the Orange Free State.

Factors in the New Imperialism.   Such was the situa-

tion in sub-Saharan Africa before the Great Colony Hunt
got under way. Though western Europe before 1870 had
shown a general apathy toward acquiring extensive colonies, this mood suddenly changed into a veritable orgy
of what we now call imperialism. It is difficult to explain satisfactorily the advent of the "white man's burden." A number of factors joined to bring about the
scramble for tropical territories. Popular journalism, now
reaching the masses for the first time, played up the
heroic and patriotic features of the explorations. The cult
of science, emergent at this time, led to a curiosity about
all strange lands. There was also a deep and sincere humanitarian movement that expressed itself in missionary work and in the belief that savage customs and
ignorance could only be rectified by European control.
Finally, there was the influence of the new industrialism
and nationalism. Expanding factories sought markets
overseas and businessmen wanted colonies where these
markets could be built without tariff interference of other
nations. At the same time these tropical lands provided
sources of valuable raw materials and an outlet for the
investment of surplus capital. Above all, the champagne
mood of nationalism thought of colonies as a manifestation of both a country's power, influence, and cultural
destiny.

    Leopold and Stanley. A shrewd monarch had been
carefully watching the progress of exploration in Africa.
In 1876 Leopold II of Belgium convened a conference at
Brussels, ostensibly to help introduce into Africa the
blessings of civilization. In his opening address Leopold
declared: "The object which unites us here to-day is one
of those which deserve in the highest degree to occupy
the friends of humanity. To open to civilization the only
part of our globe where it has not penetrated, to pierce
the darkness which envelops entire populations, is, I venture to say, a crusade worthy of this century of progress." [4] As a result of this meeting, the International African Association was founded. Gradually, however, while
this organization retained its international character,
Leopold became its master. In 1879 a separate committee

---

[4] Cited in J. Holland Rose, *The Development of the Euro-
    pean Nations* (New York, 1916) Part II, p. 268.

was set up, called the International Association of the Congo, and under the king's direction it practically superseded the original, parent organization.

Snubbed by his former countrymen in England, Stanley became Leopold's agent, and in the years 1879-1880 he made numerous treaties with chiefs in the Congo. Altogether some 900,000 square miles were obtained for the Belgian king. In most cases the African chiefs fixed their marks on the treaties with little idea that they were surrendering their lands. Later, this was the common practice of all agents of the Great Powers. (*See Reading No. 2.*) Leopold's real-estate coup precipitated among the great European powers a hectic scramble for colonies. In 1882 Britain occupied Egypt, the following year Portugal protested vigorously against Leopold's claims in the Congo region, and Germany prepared to join the Great Colony Hunt. Following her unification, Germany's trade and industry mounted rapidly. The merchants of Bremen and Hamburg carried on a brisk trade with various coastal ports in West and South-West Africa, and German missionaries expanded their activities. A newly founded Colonial Society also carried on propaganda for the acquisition of colonies, especially in Africa. The result was the raising of the German flag in South-West Africa in 1884, and with it the acquisition of a huge colony of more than 300,000 square miles. While assuring the British Government that he was not interested in territorial concessions in West Africa, the wily Bismarck arranged to send the experienced German explorer, Gustav Nachtigal, to this area. In the summer of 1884 this agent raised the German flag in Togoland, and then proceeding to the Cameroons, he hastily signed treaties with various chiefs. In this latter area a British consul, with his treaty forms, came a week too late, but did establish British supremacy along the coast in Nigeria.

Conference of Berlin. It now appeared that there might be serious rivalry between the Great Powers in Europe over the division of African territory, especially in the Congo Basin. To counter this threat, a conference of the powers was called at Berlin in 1884. Certain general rules were laid down to regulate the occupation of new African territories by the Great Powers; it was also decided to recognize the rights of the Congo Association

to much of the Congo area. The boundary claims of
France and Portugal were adjusted, thus creating the
French Congo and modern Angola as we know them to-
day. Freedom of trade and navigation was guaranteed to
all in the Congo. Above all, high-sounding declarations
were made about uplifting the natives, spreading the
Gospel, and stamping out slavery. (*See Reading No. 3.*)
We will see shortly how these objectives were carried out.

Following the Berlin Conference the partition of Africa
proceeded at a hectic pace so that by 1902 all of the sub-
Saharan continent had been parceled out among the
powers except the diminutive Republic of Liberia. Four
nations were the participants in this final phase of rivalry:
Britain, France, Germany, and Italy. The first two came
out with the lion's share—more than three million square
miles each—with Britain controlling by far the largest
population and the most valuable economic resources.
Germany secured an African empire of about one million
square miles, but Italy was disastrously defeated by an
Abyssinian army in 1896, ending her imperial dreams for
the moment in this area, and had to content herself with
two petty morsels in East Africa—Eritrea and Italian
Somaliland.

British, French and German Rivalries. This partition of the African continent was attended by serious Big
Power rivalries. At the end of 1884, while the Berlin
Conference was in session, a German colonial enthusiast,
Karl Peters, and two companions left Europe on a cloak-
and-dagger mission. Proceeding to the African mainland
opposite Zanzibar, this trio, armed with suitable treaty
blanks, obtained the signatures of numerous chiefs who
unknowingly gave up the rights to their ancient lands.
A German East African Association was formed to
develop the region of some 300,000 square miles, and in
1885 the German Government announced a protectorate
over the region obtained by Karl Peters. To meet this
threat a group of British businessmen interested in the
development of East Africa began to make treaties with
the native chiefs in the Kenya area. These men later
formed the British Imperial East African Association to
safeguard their interests. Despite the protests of the Sultan of Zanzibar, who long had held a sovereignty over the
East African coast and its hinterland, the German Gov-

ernment refused to be budged from its position. Britain refused to support the Sultan and in two agreements (1886 and 1890) amicably settled all points of contention between the two European states. Boundaries were formalized both in West and in East Africa. The Germans retained the huge area known as the German East Africa Protectorate—to be named Tanganyika after 1919; the British were allotted their East Africa Protectorate, later to be known as Kenya Colony, together with a protectorate over Uganda. The Sultan of Zanzibar also recognized Britain as his suzerain.

To Britain, French rivalry was more dangerous than German. From about 1871 French soldiers and explorers carried the tricolor throughout most of West Africa. Penetrating far east into the open lands of the Sudan, the French then turned south to the coast and the sea. The densely forested area between Liberia and the Gold Coast became the French Ivory Coast Protectorate by 1893. In 1892 the notorious kingdom of Dahomey, with its bloodthirsty rulers, came under firm French control. All of the vast hinterland of West Africa was ruled from Paris. Gambia, the Gold Coast, and Sierra Leone—British Colonies—were small enclaves in this vast empire of France. Only in Nigeria did the British manage to push back into the interior and secure a magnificent colony. In Nigeria both France and England were on the verge of war on several occasions. And as elsewhere in British Africa it was a private trading company, the Royal Niger Company under its able leader, Sir George Taubman Goldie, that was instrumental in blocking French expansion. Treaties made in 1890 and 1898 between France and Britain settled these Niger rivalries; but scarcely were the signatures dry when a new crisis arose in the valley of the Nile in eastern Sudan. France entertained a dream of empire whereby she would control a solid block of territory running across Africa from the Atlantic Ocean to the Red Sea. To claim eastern Sudan, Colonel Marchand was sent on a hazardous expedition. It took him from the French Congo to Fashoda on the Nile, which was reached in July, 1898. A few weeks later General Kitchener arrived and in the name of Britain demanded the withdrawal of Marchand. France and Britain were on the brink of war. Some tense months passed, but in the spring of 1899 France gave way, leaving Britain in possession of the upper Nile Valley.

South African War. Just as France had her dream of a great empire extending east to west across Africa, so Great Britain planned for her "Cape-to-Cairo" corridor. This was mainly the dream of Cecil Rhodes (1853-1902), one of the most remarkable men of modern times. Shrewd, ruthless, and inordinately ambitious, this titan dominated the history of South Africa in the closing years of the nineteenth century. It was Rhodes who was responsible for Britain taking over Bechuanaland, a strategic corridor linking Cape Colony with the rich valley of the Zambezi. Like Taubman Goldie, Rhodes used a chartered company, the British South Africa Company, to extend British influence north of South Africa. Securing a treaty from the powerful Matabele chief, Lobengula, Rhodes proceeded to take over this native's territories of Mashonaland and Matabeleland. In 1890 the company sent a flying column into the area to begin development and settlement. Thus modern Rhodesia was born. The British nailed down their control of East Central Africa by extending a protectorate over Nyasaland in 1889.

Rhodes' ambitions had been realized in the Zambezi valley, but in South Africa proper he was not so fortunate. It will be recalled that the Boers had trekked north to escape from foreign tutelage. But the affairs of Boer and Briton still continued to be mixed up. The discovery of diamonds in 1868 and of gold in 1884 brought tens of thousands of immigrants. In the Transvaal in a single decade half of the population consisted of newcomers, mainly British, who paid nearly all the taxes and owned one third of the land. It had been apparent since the 1850's to some British statesmen and even to some Dutch that the only solution in South Africa was federation. Only in this way could a common native policy be framed and conflicting interests in tariffs and railways be reconciled. Several attempts were made by the British to interest the two Boer states in some form of union with the two British colonies, but these failed.

In the 1890's Boer-British relations rapidly deteriorated. The patriotic but unbending president of the Transvaal, Paul Kruger, detested the ways and objectives of the British—the *Uitlanders*—in his midst. He taxed them heavily, refused to provide adequate schools, denied them the vote, and obstructed their acquisition of citizenship. As rebellion began to take shape among the *Uitlanders,* who petitioned the Queen for redress of their grievances, Rhodes, ever impatient, tried to set off a rebellion in Johannesburg by a madcap expedition of his armed police from Rhodesia. This Jameson Raid was a failure, Rhodes suffered serious disgrace, and the Boers more than ever set their hearts against their unwanted guests. Meanwhile the British Government had become alarmed at the growth of German influence in the Transvaal. Military advisers were secured from Berlin by Kruger and large amounts of military matériel were bought from Germany. Great Britain began to augment her armed strength in Cape Colony and Natal while at the same time fruitless negotiations were carried on with the Boers.

In 1899 the expected conflict occurred. Kruger issued an ultimatum to Britain to withdraw her troops. On her refusal the forces of the two republics invaded the British colonies. At first outnumbered, the British rushed in reinforcements, but were surprised at the fighting prowess of the Boer commandos. Finally in 1902 after desperate resistance the Boers had to give way before the greater strength of the British Empire. Peace was signed at Vereeniging in 1902. The British were very generous. There were no indemnities, and a large sum of money was given to the Boers to restock their farms and rehabilitate their country. In 1907 the Orange Free State and the Transvaal were given self-government. And in 1909 these joined with the two British colonies to form the completely free Dominion of the Union of South Africa. Briton and Boer at last were united to face the common problems of South Africa.

Organization and Development of Colonies. By 1902 the scramble for Africa was over, the extent of the main colonial empires had been fixed. In the closing years of the nineteenth and the first decade of the twentieth century, the colonial powers occupied themselves with establishing peace, setting up administrative machinery, and constructing communications. Commerce was developed, and in East and Central Africa, both in British and German possessions, European settlement was started.

The Scandal of the Congo.   On the whole European rule was enlightened. At first, German administration was too military and harsh, and a number of serious revolts took place in the German colonies. The most serious blot, however, occurred against the white man's burden in the Congo Free State. Despite the high-sounding pronouncements of the Berlin Act, King Leopold II exploited his Congo possessions solely for his profit, regardless of the consequences to the Africans. In ten years he squeezed at least fifteen million dollars out of the Congo by forcing the natives to produce rubber and other products. The natives suffered heavy taxes, beatings, and forced labor and frequently were murdered. The Congo became a veritable hell on earth. (*See Reading No. 4.*) In 1903 the British Government proposed an investigation, while missionary circles raised their voices against the crimes of the Congo. The Government of the United States also became aroused. Finally, Leopold was forced to turn over his vast holdings to Belgium, whose parliament now sought to undo the terrible harm done to the Congo natives. A mercenary promoter to the end, Leopold induced the parliament to compensate him handsomely for his "sacrifice" of the Congo.

— 3 —

AFRICA EMERGENT: TWO WORLD WARS AND AFTER

World War Comes to Africa.   In the summer of 1914 the era—more than a decade—of tension, diplomatic crisis, and feverish rearmament culminated in world war. In September at a special session, the Union parliament

joined Britain in the struggle against Germany and the
Central Powers. This decision was hotly opposed by the
Boer diehards, who detested all things British and had
never been reconciled to the defeat of 1902. The commander of the army, General Beyers, resigned his post,
asserting that the German treatment of the Belgians was
no worse than British acts of barbarism during the Boer
War. To this charge General Smuts, who with his chief
Botha was the great exponent of cooperation between
Boer and Briton, replied in a letter: "You forget to mention that since the South African War the British people
gave South Africa her entire freedom under a constitution which makes it possible for us to realise our national
ideals along our own lines, and which, incidentally, al-
lows you to write a letter for which you would, without
doubt, be liable in the German Empire to the supreme
penalty." [5] Rebellion against the government nevertheless
broke out. The South African prime minister supported
by his colleague Smuts quickly crushed the revolt in a
few months. The great majority of the white population,
both Boer and Briton, loyally supported the war effort.

Elsewhere in Africa the German colonies were on the
defensive. Cut off from the fatherland, they could not
secure needed military supplies and fighting men. Togoland was invaded by French and British forces and had
to surrender in a few weeks. The Cameroons held out
for a year and a half. Then, outnumbered and without
ammunition, the small German army crossed safely to
the neutral sanctuary of Rio Muni, Spanish territory.
General Botha, a hero of the South African War and
now head of the South African Government, commanded
forty thousand troops as he attacked German South-
West Africa. The campaign was a struggle with nature.
Roads and railroads were scarce, and the terrain was
barren and scorching hot. After stiff resistance the German army was compelled to surrender in July 1915. The
campaign in German East Africa was one of the heroic
sagas of World War I. Its defense was in the hands of a
resourceful young staff officer, General von Lettow Vor-
beck, who had three thousand European troops and
eleven thousand native askari in his army. Initial at-

[5] Lord Elton, *Imperial Commonwealth* (New York, 1946)
p. 476.

tempts to conquer the territory by Britain were failures, and in 1916 General Smuts was given command. By the end of the year German strength had been scattered and the struggle now continued as a guerrilla war. Finally, in November 1917 a tattered remnant of troops under their commander retreated into Portuguese territory and managed to remain intact until peace was declared in November 1918.

German Colonies and the Peace Settlement. The victorious Allies were committed to the "free, open-minded and absolutely impartial adjustment of all colonial claims." This was one of President Wilson's Fourteen Points. But during the war and while the peace conference was in session a chorus of denunciation was leveled against German colonial rule. This indictment contained words like "cruel," "brutal," "arrogant," and "lustful." Objectivity also seems to be a casualty of war. All colonial possessions, therefore, were taken from Germany and distributed among the Allies. In the view of experts on this question the charges against Germany as a colonial power were distorted. It is true that in the first phase of her rule there was harshness, and in consequence some native revolts. But by 1914 German policy had become both humane and progressive, and in the application of science to colonial development the Germans were unsurpassed.

The German colonies, however, were not simply annexed. During the war there had been much talk about the well-being of the native peoples and the internationalization of colonies under some world authority. Words such as "trusteeship" and "mandate" were used, referring to the responsibility of advanced nations for the welfare of backward peoples in their charge. At the peace conference General Smuts was largely the father of what came to be the mandate system, but he also obtained valuable suggestions from such American experts as Walter Lippmann and George Louis Beer. Quite a struggle ensued as the issue of ex-enemy colonies and possessions was resolved. The result was a compromise in which, while the principle of internationalization was given some recognition, the victors to all intents and purposes obtained practical control of the colonies.

The Mandate System. Article 22 of the Covenant

of the League of Nations defined the mandate system. (*See Reading No. 5.*) The keynote of its provisions was that the "well-being and development" of these backward colonial lands form a "sacred trust of civilization." A commission appointed by the Allied Powers to draft all mandates, except those in the Middle East, met in London in the summer of 1919. After considerable delay the mandate for South-West Africa was approved at the end of 1920 and the other African Mandates in the middle of 1922. Great Britain received the all-important mandate for East Africa, now known as Tanganyika. (*See Reading No. 6.*) All mandatory powers had to present an annual report of their administration and were accountable to the League's Permanent Mandates Commission. Togoland was divided into British and French mandates, as were the Cameroons; and a small area of western Tanganyika, Ruanda-Urundi, was turned over to Belgium for mandate. As for South-West Africa, since it was adjacent to and had been conquered by the Union of South Africa, it was natural that the mandate be given to that country.

In all these African mandates the administering power was pledged to respect the basic rights of the natives. Slavery was to be stamped out where it had lingered on, there was to be no militarization of the African natives, and compulsory labor was to be utilized only for public projects and with adequate compensation. The rights of Africans in their land was to be scrupulously respected and the open door, economically, was guaranteed to all members of the League. This last, by preventing monopolies and other exclusive practices, would help to prevent the African from being exploited economically. Finally, as basic rights, Africans were to enjoy the benefit of widening services in education and public health.

To supervise the administration of these rights the Permanent Mandates Commission met annually in Geneva. Among its personnel were some of the most distinguished authorities in colonial administration. In effect the commission was only an advisory body. It could not send out its own investigators to a mandate, it could not summon witnesses from a mandate, and all petitions had to pass through the hands of the affected mandatory power, which in turn tendered the petition with its comments to the commission. Finally, it was quite beyond the power of this body to deprive a nation of its mandate.

Because of these shortcomings there was considerable criticism of the League mandate system in the 1920's and 1930's. While some criticism was justifiable, it was quite untrue to charge that the mandate system was completely ineffectual. As the late Professor P. T. Moon put it: "The mandate system may be toothless, but it is not bootless." The Mandate Commission was a widely respected body. Its proof and praise when given were not ignored. The policy of trusteeship that it supported profoundly influenced colonial administration. As the French minister of colonies said in 1923: "Reforms accomplished in one place will inevitably penetrate elsewhere. Whether we like it or not, colonial questions have ceased to be purely national; they have become international, placed under the eyes of the world." [6]

The New Emphasis on African Studies. The principle of international trusteeship and the influence of the Mandates Commission helped to advance in the 1920's a trend recognizing the need of scientific knowledge about colonial peoples in general and Africans in particular. Up to this time there had been much misunderstanding and many mistakes in the treatment of colonial people because of the lack of precise information about their institutions and traditional ways of life. A new branch of the social sciences, however, now appeared, known as social anthropology. It concerned "the study of the diffusion of Western cultures among primitive peoples," with what one of its founders so well termed "the anthropology of the changing native." In particular, great advances were made in African studies. The International Institute of African Languages and Cultures, founded in 1926, did notable work in this field. (*See Reading No. 7.*) It sponsored the study of the many African languages, prepared school books in the various vernaculars, donated prizes for the best books written in indigenous languages by Africans, and supported active anthropological research in the African colonies.

As part of this new emphasis upon African studies, the

[6] Cited in Parker Thomas Moon, *Imperialism and World Politics* (The Macmillan Co., New York, 1944) p. 512. By permission of The Macmillan Company.

University of Cape Town established in 1918 a School of African Life and Languages, and in various British universities chairs of social anthropology were created. At the same time African subjects were stressed at Cambridge and Oxford Universities and at the London School of Economics. In France a number of societies and journals devoted their attention to African subjects, as did the École Coloniale. The Museum of the Belgian Congo issued valuable monographs on African subjects, and special courses were offered in the same field at the University of Louvain and the Colonial University of Antwerp. In Germany valuable investigations in African anthropology were carried on at various universities. Even in the United States, a country not directly concerned with problems of native policy and administration, a number of anthropologists, such as Professor Herskovits, turned their attention to Africa. And for the first time the governments of the various colonies in Africa engaged anthropologists to carry out investigations or diverted able colonial officers to do this work. Anthropology had become the indispensable handmaid of colonial government. What might be thought of as the new science of African studies came of age in 1938 with the publication of Lord Hailey's monumental *An African Survey: A Study of Problems Arising in Africa South of the Sahara*. General Smuts in the Rhodes Memorial Lecture given in 1929 had stressed the necessity of such a survey; and later with the support of the Carnegie Corporation of New York and the Rhodes Trust, Lord Hailey, a distinguished British colonial authority, was able to direct the survey.

Enlightened Native Policy. All this discussion and study of African affairs had a salutary effect on the various colonial powers endeavoring to clarify their native policies in the direction of protecting the interests of the African people. Britain was especially active in this regard. In 1923 the clash of interests between the immigrant Europeans and East Indians in the East African colony of Kenya caused the British Government to issue an official white paper in which it was stated that if the interests of immigrant communities and those of the African came into conflict, the former must prevail. This statement of native policy came to be known as *paramountcy*. (*See Reading No. 8.*)

In 1921 a British colonial official who had played a
notable part in the acquisition of colonies in both East
and West Africa, and who had set his imprint on the
methods and philosophy of native rule in Africa, published a book that exercised wide influence. This was
The Dual Mandate in British Tropical Africa by Sir F. D.
(later Lord) Lugard. In this volume the concept of the
dual mandate is defined and defended. The author argues
that the colonial powers can and should administer their
possessions both for the native peoples concerned and
for their own people and the world in general. In other
words, the mandate is to raise the standard of living of
the African peoples by making available for the outside
world the rich tropical products of the dependencies. (*See
Reading No. 9.*) An application of Lugard's doctrine was
that while the concept of native paramountcy must be
adhered to, in areas like Kenya the so-called dual policy
should be followed. This was defined by the British
Government as "the complementary development of native and nonnative communities." The dual policy rested
on the assumption that European contact with the African
would stimulate his progress. Hence, in the 1920's and
1930's the British Government gave moderate support
to white settlement in areas climatically suited to their
residence. (*See Reading No. 10.*)

Closely connected with the formulation of humanitarian and positive principles in native policy was a com-
parable movement in African education. Under the
auspices of the British Colonial Office and with the cooperation of various missionary bodies, the Advisory Committee on Native Education in the British Tropical Dependencies issued a significant memorandum in 1925 defining
the scope and objectives of education in tropical Africa.
This committee declared "that education should be
adapted to the mentality, aptitudes, occupations and
traditions of the various peoples, conserving as far as
possible all sound and healthy elements in the fabric of
their social life. . . . Its aim should be to render the
individual more efficient in his or her condition of life.
. . . It must include the raising up of capable, trust-
worthy, public-spirited leaders of the people. . . . As
resources permit, the door of advancement, through higher
education, in Africa must be increasingly opened for

those who by character, ability and temperament show themselves fitted to profit by such education."

While the British Colonial Office was exploring the needs of the African people in schooling, a well-known American educational and philanthropic foundation was sponsoring all-important field investigations of educational conditions and needs in tropical Africa. In 1920-1921, a commission headed by Dr. Thomas Jesse Jones, Educational Director of the Phelps-Stokes Fund, studied native education in West, South, and Equatorial Africa. A challenging report was published under Phelps-Stokes auspices in 1922. Two years later the fund, in cooperation with the International Education Board, sent a commission to East Africa and another report on native educational needs was the result.

African Economic Developments. As various learned, governmental, and missionary bodies became increasingly interested in native policy and the requisite knowledge for intelligent action by colonial authorities in Africa, so businessmen became vitally aware of the tremendous potentialities of the Dark Continent that was rapidly losing this shady color. Africa south of the Sahara in 1885 had no roads, mines, factories, or railways —the only exception being South Africa. There was no native capital and there were substantial obstacles to economic advancement, such as inadequate rainfall in many areas, deadly enemies to human health, and the fact that the Africans possessed practically no civilization as we are accustomed to use this term. They had no body of scientific data, little accumulated knowledge of the past, and no productive technology worthy of the name.

Between 1885 and 1914 substantial if not spectacular progress was made in building railroads, opening up mines, and starting plantations. The tempo quickened in the 1920's: the Union of South Africa developed its mines and agriculture; European settlement advanced in the salubrious highlands of Kenya and Southern Rhodesia; amazing developments in mining took place in Northern Rhodesia and the Belgian Congo; and under an enlightened colonial rule the native farmers of British West Africa produced a tremendous quantity of cocoa and palm oil. It should be clearly understood that without outside capital, economic development in tropical

Africa is next to impossible. By the mid-1930's, it was estimated, a little more than five billion dollars had been invested in African enterprises; and almost one third of this sum had been used to build railways.

In the gross aggregate of world trade Africa was not important; south of the Sahara the continent's trade amounted only to 2.8% of the world exports and 2.6% of its imports. But the importance of Africa was the concentration and even monopoly of its production in certain key commodities. For example, in world gold production it produced 56% of the entire supply, in chrome ore 50%, in radium and vanadium another 50%; and copper production in the late 1930's reached 22% of the world's supply. In the following products, as the figures indicate, African production in the world was decisive: 93% of the palm oil, 62% of the cocoa, and more than 90% of all the diamonds and cobalt.

As the economic importance of the African territories became increasingly clear, Germany raised an impatient voice for the return of her ex-colonies taken by the Treaty of Versailles in 1919. She had never become reconciled to the loss of her empire as indicated by the fact that a large wreath inscribed to "The Colonies" had been conspicuous in the Hall of Generals in Munich ever since the signing of the treaty. In the next decade a steady barrage of histories, articles, and novels appeared in Germany on the colonies. Courses in colonial administration were given in the universities, and ex-colonial officials formed societies devoted to the objective of regaining her colonies for Germany. In particular, Dr. Heinrich Schnee, a former colonial governor, wrote numerous articles on this question. In 1926 his important book *German Colonization, Past and Present* was published in English.

Germany Demands Colonies. The impact of world depression gave a new twist to Germany's demand for her colonies. Originally, the colonial question was largely a matter of honor, the necessity to rectify the "myth of colonial guilt." With depression and its resulting unemployment, loss of foreign markets, and above all, lack of foreign exchange—British pounds and American dollars—to buy raw materials, the Germans began to demand back their colonies as indispensable for economic recovery. (*See Reading No. 11.*) After the rise of Hitlerian Nazism, the campaign for the colonies rose to a crescendo. Germany must have colonies to have easy access to raw materials; she must have room to expand, she must have her own markets for goods and investments. The Third Reich was joined in this chorus by Italy and Japan, who, too, demanded their place in the sun.

In Germany in 1934 there were nation-wide ceremonies celebrating the birth of colonial empire in Africa just half a century before. General Hermann Göring was the first Nazi cabinet officer to make a public demand for the return of the colonies, and in 1939 Hitler made colonial revision the main theme of his famous January speech. This "Have and Have-Not Business," as it was called, brought forth a deluge of controversy—in the press, in legislatures, and in numerous books. A novel written by Hans Grimm, *Nation without Room,* first published in the early 1920's, became widely popular during the Nazi regime. There were many echoes of the colonial question in Africa. German settlers in Tanganyika, confident of Hitler's success, became strident in their demands to be returned to the fatherland. On the other hand, British settlers in this territory and also in contiguous territories of Britain were equally vehement in their protestations that there should be no surrender to the Third Reich. In all this debate, the basic questions in Africa were lost sight of: How best could Africa's economic resources be developed and the standard of its people raised? How should its people be assisted in both throwing off the incubus of superstition and barbaric customs and taking over the best elements in Western culture? And how could the African people be given experience in political responsibility and be prepared for self-government?

Africa's Role in World War II. The Second World War fully revealed the strategic and economic importance of Africa. When Italy joined forces with the Axis, the Mediterranean life-line of France and Britain to the Near and Far East was seriously obstructed. At the same time, the fall of France meant the loss of French North and West Africa with their vital military installations and airfields. Another serious loss was Japan's seizure of the rich colonies of the democracies with their vital raw tropical materials. These setbacks meant that the airfields of British West Africa became of extreme importance in a new communications route across the continent. The ports of Freetown, Cape Town, Durban, and Mombasa also became vital for convoys carrying heavy equipment to Egypt and the Persian Gulf. Finally, the United States and the Western democracies became urgently dependent upon such raw materials as copper, chromite, iron, manganese, sisal, gold, tea and coffee, cotton, and radium—all produced in substantial quantities in Africa.

The people of the British African colonies remained loyal. As Africans, their educated leaders had little love for Hitler's theories of racialism and the stigmas put on the black race. In East Africa native troops were increased from a peacetime 11,000 to 228,000, and in British West Africa the corresponding figures were 8,000 and 146,000. These African troops played a significant part in gaining ultimate victory: they fought in Somaliland and Ethiopia against the Italians and later took part in the difficult jungle fighting against the Japanese in Burma. In the Belgian Congo the authorities did not accept King Leopold's surrender, but sent out this message on the radio: "The war is to go on." Congolese Africans were recruited for an expanded defense force which rendered good service to the Allied cause. One event was the trek of a Congolese force, 1400 miles across Africa to Abyssinia, where it helped to defeat an Italian army. In French Africa the armistice signed on June 22, 1940, with Hitler brought about a period of confusion. West Africa supported the Vichy regime and its leader Pétain; it also accepted Axis military commissions. In August, however, Felix Eboué, the Negro governor of the Chad region, proclaimed his support of De Gaulle and his Free French in London. Other colonies in the Federation of French Equatorial Africa joined, although there was some resistance in Gabon. By the middle of 1943 all of the French colonies in Africa, and indeed in the empire except Indochina, had united with General de Gaulle. As in the case of the Congolese, the Free French fought heroically against Axis forces. In the Union of South Africa, war brought dissension and uncertainty. There were strong elements that were not only anti-British but also pro-Nazi. General Smuts, however, was determined to support Britain and her allies and forced the resignation of General Hertzog as prime minister. Taking this post, Smuts flung himself into the war effort, sending two divisions to fight in Libya and Abyssinia and a third to Italy.

While Free French, Congolese, British West and East Africans, Rhodesians, and South Africans did their stint at the front, their people on the home front worked feverishly to produce the necessary military installations and raw materials. A string of airfields was built across West Africa and as many as two to three hundred planes stopped at the Accra airfield in a single day. The African territories also poured out a rich harvest of supplies for the foundries of Britain and the United States—rubber, tin, palm oil, copper, chrome, and iron.

Impact of the War on Colonial Rule. World War II accelerated interest in the destiny of Africa and a new sense of responsibility on the part of the colonial powers for the welfare and advancement of its peoples. At the same time there was widespread denunciation of colonialism and imperialism as causes of war and the means of selfish exploitation of backward people. Some of this criticism was justified, but much was loose talk without benefit of facts. At any rate this anticolonialism did spur the imperial powers to quicken their efforts to improve their rule and justify it before the world. The enunciation of the Atlantic Charter in August 1941 did much to quicken the formulation of plans for the advancement of colonial peoples. (*See Readings Nos. 12 and 13.*) At the same time the colonial people were led to expect grand vistas of self-government and economic prosperity. Before 1939 the colonial powers in Africa and elsewhere had followed a policy of *laissez faire*. Their belief had been that government responsibility was to maintain order and enforce the law but to keep out of matters of economics, welfare, and social policy. The tragic condition of some of the colonies during the world depression of the early 1930's had helped to focus attention upon the poverty, illiteracy, disease, and misery of many of the backward people of the tropics. In Britain there was much criticism against what were called "the colonial slums."

In 1940 Britain introduced a new and bold policy of

economic development for her colonies. Its Colonial Development and Welfare Act was "to make provision for the development of the resources of Colonies, protectorates, protected states and mandated territories, and the welfare of their peoples." This act provided for the expenditure of £5,000,000 a year for ten years, with an additional £500,000 available for research. In 1945 another act was passed providing for the expenditure from British funds of £120,000,000 in ten years; in 1955 the latest Development Act provided for a new sum of £80,000,000 in the years 1955-1960. These substantial sums from the British Treasury are joined with funds raised by the local colonial governments. After 1945 the British Colonial Office requested each colony in Africa and elsewhere to prepare a ten-year plan of development in such fields as agriculture, communications, education, health, and housing.

Declarations on New Colonial Policies. In the House of Commons in July 1943 the British Colonial Secretary summed up the new policy for the dependencies thus: "We are pledged to guide Colonial peoples along the road to self-government within the framework of the British Empire. We are pledged to build up their social and economic institutions, and we are pledged to develop their natural resources." One of the most significant features of the new British concept of colonial responsibility was the emphasis upon economic development— the realization that political advances necessitate an adequate economic base. From every quarter in Britain came plans and statements on colonial reform. (*See Readings Nos. 14 and 15.*)

Other colonial powers issued declarations on colonial aims—all in the direction of political reforms, and most such declarations promising economic development. In December 1942 the Queen of the Netherlands announced that a Netherlands Commonwealth would be set up after the war on a "solid foundation of complete partnership" in which there would be "no room for discrimination according to race or nationality." In January 1944 a most significant conference was held at Brazzaville, French Equatorial Africa. The attitude underlying this meeting, as officially described, was: "The chief aim of the colonial policy of the new France will be to ensure

the material and moral development of the natives . . .
while respecting their culture and civilization and having
them participate, within the framework of a French
Federation, in the evolution of Metropolitan France."
(*See Reading No. 16.*)

Between 1939 and 1945 there was much discussion on
the desirability of the various colonial powers' cooperat-
ing in the fields of health, communications, education,
agriculture, etc. This would be especially desirable in
contiguous areas such as French and British West Africa.
The idea was put forth to establish regional commissions
to direct common research, medical, educational, and
economic development. (*See Reading No. 17.*) Colonial
regionalism, as it was known, was begun in the West
Indies when Britain and the United States set up the
Anglo-American Caribbean Commission. This arrangement was extended in 1945 when France and the
Netherlands joined the organization. While this idea of
regionalism after the war did not fulfill the expectations
of many of its initial supporters—for it did not lead to
any colonial power's surrendering its sovereignty to an
international regional commission—it has nevertheless
brought about much valuable working together of colonial governments. In Africa, for example, there have
been many conferences on education, labor, communications, food and nutrition, and other subjects. In 1950
in a meeting held in Paris, it was agreed to set up a
commission for technical cooperation of all governments
south of the Sahara. The idea for a scientific council for
this area was also indorsed.

European Impact and the Changing African. It is
now time to observe what fifty to seventy years of
European contact have done with the African. (In South
Africa, of course, the period has been much longer.)
This impact of the West on the African way of life is
one of the great transformations of modern times, especially when one considers its speed. The African is
leaving the ways of the *kraal* (native village) much faster
than our European ancestors forsook those of the
medieval manor. In fact, a revolution is taking place in
Africa in a single generation which in Europe took a
century or two. The main agents of this Western impact
can be easily identified. The white man's government

levies taxes, forcing the African either to grow a money crop for sale, or more usually, to go and work for some white employer. New rules must be obeyed—there can be no more cattle stealing or raiding against a traditional tribal enemy. Above all, the land in many colonies is no longer open. Definite areas are made into native reserves where alone the African has land rights. In addition to government, there are the mines, plantations, and farms. Sometimes the African can bring his family and find employment as a squatter on a European farm. Most usually, however, he leaves his family behind and comes to the mine and plantation as a migrant worker. Closely related to these agents of impact is the city. Here the African obtains employment as a servant in a European home; he works in some great hotel or performs menial work in a factory. But whatever he does, he is pouring into such cities as Dakar, Lagos, Nairobi, Leopoldville, and above all, Johannesburg, by the thousands. Another important Western agent of change is the Christian missionary, for in the past he has been the main agency bringing Western education to the African. There can be no lament for the passing of the indigenous religious beliefs and customs in Africa. In the new life that is opening up for Africans, only Christianity can provide the moral basis for reasonable and civilized action. But it is easier to destroy the old faiths than to make the new an integral and meaningful part of life. Many Africans have given up their old gods, but they do not truly understand or deeply feel the new religion they have embraced.

The African admires the power, wealth, and diversity of Western civilization. He is entranced by its gadgets, cars, and airplanes. The African who by contact with the European way of life becomes "detribalized" is eager to cast aside his tribal loyalties and ties. The result is often confusion and frustration, for the new civilization he seeks does not have the simplicity and certainty of the old. As Professor Macmillan has put it: "It is a misfortune that civilization today offers no clear-cut system of ideas for Africans to follow, no creed such as Christianity or Islam once offered with confidence, no simple and thrilling rule of life for the convert from barbarism to embrace, hardly even a civic system of which he can feel himself a part." [7] Often he feels "above" the old life he has cut adrift from, but he is not given status or a place in the new world to which he wants to belong. The result naturally is trouble. This comes in the form of the breaking down of family ties and the growth of bad habits in the city such as drunkenness and gang warfare. Above all, it means an alarming increase in crime in the cities.

It is certainly incorrect to think of the pre-European period in Africa in terms of a Rousseau-like society peopled with noble savages. There can be few regrets for the old life; it had to be superseded, for it was cruel, limited, static, and violent. Like all great historical movements, changing Africa is an age of confused transition. To many it has brought opportunity and the good life; to many more it has brought sorrow and regret. This is because the movement is proceeding so fast and by an unplanned route.

The Rise of African Nationalism. Nationalism in Africa is one of the most important results of the impact of Western culture. The African learns of the democratic system of government enjoyed by his colonial officials in Europe. Or in the case of South Africa, he sees a parliamentary system functioning in his own country—but only for white men. The two decades separating World War I from World War II were the formative years of African nationalism. On the surface, little was to be seen, but pressures and aspirations were building up that broke loose with astonishing force following the end of hostilities in 1945. In the twenty years before 1939 there were hardly any manifestations of African nationalism except in the British colonies. Such movements as the Nigerian National Democratic Party, the West African National Congress, and the Young Kikuyu Association in Kenya evidenced the birth of a new political consciousness. In the Union of South Africa an African National Congress was formed as early as 1913. And outside of Africa various Negro leaders and intellectuals were sponsoring a Pan-African movement which had its first meeting in Paris in 1919. Dr. W. E. Burghardt DuBois, from the United States, was one of

[7] W. M. Macmillan, *Africa Emergent* (Harmondsworth, 1939) pp. 67-68.

its most influential members. Other Pan-African conferences followed, the last being held in Manchester, England, in 1945. These meetings supported the principle of
self-determination for the African and insisted upon
measures being taken to ensure his social and economic
betterment.

If the seeds of African nationalism were sown in the
two decades between wars, they matured with astonishing
speed after 1939. A number of factors explain this growth.
To justify their cause the Allied nations, such as Britain,
France, and the United States, promised to speed up the
tempo of self-government for colonial peoples. A host of
orators made rather sweeping statements about prosperity
and full stomachs for all after victory was achieved.
One detects a note of sarcasm in this Englishman's statement on the promise of Utopia for all: "And finally there
was launched amongst the colonial peoples a barrage of
propaganda on the necessity to beat Hitler because of
Hitler's racism, accompanied by promises about the
Century of the Common Man, and perspectives of Fords
and Frigidaires and Freedoms for all the little people." [8]
Some assurance to colonial people that new efforts would
be made to ensure their economic and political advancement was necessary and overdue; what was regrettable
was the loose and even reckless promise of freedom from
practically all the old problems, no matter what they
might be. Other factors supporting colonial nationalism
were the decline in the prestige of the white man following his defeats at the hands of Japan; the loss of his
power both material and spiritual in the days of appeasement and in the initial reverses at the hands of the Axis
armies; and finally, the inflation and wartime shortages
which created discontent and fanned grievances among
the Africans. As we have already seen, thousands of
African troops served overseas. Their horizons were
lifted; they acquired new skills and a feeling of confidence
in their own powers. After demobilization, these ex-
soldiers expected opportunities for their new skills. As a
British *Report* observed: "The problem of turning these
war-time acquisitions to peace-time account was one that
confronted every Colonial administration in Africa."

[8] W. R. Crocker, *Self-Government for the Colonies* (London,
1949) p. 18.

Africa and the United Nations Trusteeship System.
It was not only World War II that focused attention on
colonial policy and the political aspirations of the African,
but also the establishment of a new trusteeship system
for all colonies. This was built on the experience of the
old mandate system of the League of Nations. The
Charter of the United Nations contained a "colonial
Magna Carta" in which all powers administering colonies
"recognize the principle that the interests of the inhabitants of these territories are paramount, and accept as a
sacred trust the obligation to promote to the utmost . . .
the well-being of the inhabitants of these territories." The
colonial powers specifically pledged themselves to develop
self-government and the resources of their territories. It
was further agreed that they would regularly transmit
data on their rule to the Trusteeship Council, the body
created to administer the new system. With the exception
of South-West Africa, administered by the Union of
South Africa, all the former mandates became trust
territories, and each administering nation signed an
agreement outlining the terms and conditions under which
the territory was to be administered. (*See Reading No.
18.*) The international supervision for these trust territories is stronger than that under the League of Nation's
mandate system. Petitions may be received from the
territories; in fact, individuals may present petitions in
person to the Trusteeship Council, and visiting missions
may inspect and report on conditions in the trust territories.

In Africa south of the Sahara there are six trust territories:

UNITED NATIONS TRUST TERRITORIES

Territory	Administer-ing Auth.	Popula-tion	Area (square miles)
Cameroons	United Kingdom	1,400,000	34,081
Togoland	United Kingdom	410,000	13,040
Tanganyika	United Kingdom	7,946,000	362,688
Togoland	France	1,029,946	21,236
Cameroons	France	3,076,568	166,797
Ruanda-Urundi	Belgium	4,109,000	20,916

On the basis of petitions received, reports presented by the administering powers, and reports made by the visiting missions, the Trusteeship Council makes its recommendations to the various administering powers. Furthermore, the Trusteeship Council submits its annual report to the General Assembly, where it is debated at length.

Like all aspects of the United Nations and because of the complexity of the problem, the impact of the trusteeship system has been good and bad, both encouraging and alarming. From the beginning of the United Nations, colonial subjects in general and not least Africa have been increasingly subjects for debate. From the beginning the noncolonial powers, which outnumber 52 to 8 those with dependencies, have been endeavoring to extend the United Nations authority over all colonies, not only those which come under the authority of the Trusteeship Council and the Assembly. This has occasioned many bitter debates. Furthermore, there have been numerous irresponsible attacks on the record of the various colonial powers. (*See Reading No. 19.*) While some of the recommendations of the visiting missions have been well taken and have caused administering nations to take positive action, there are others that appear unrealistic and even mischievous in their effect. In this last category one could place the recent recommendation calling for self-government in Tanganyika in less than twenty years.

The upshot of the impact of the United Nations in summary form can be stated thus: (1) It has undoubtedly focused attention on African problems. (2) The debates and criticisms have kept colonial powers on their toes, ready to justify and explain their rule; this is true not only in the trust territories proper but in all dependent territories. (3) It has in some areas encouraged the political aspirations of the Africans and in the case of South Africa stiffened the will of both Indians and Africans to resist laws that these people consider to be unjust. (4) Invaluable service is being rendered by the collection of voluminous material on the social and economic conditions of the various African territories. (5) The last comment is a serious weakness. Attacks have been made against various colonial powers by nations whose motives lie outside consideration for the wellbeing of dependent peoples. The motives are part and parcel of various national interests operating in the present field of international rivalries, whether it be the cold war, the policy of neutralism, or accumulated resentments of recently emancipated dependent peoples against their former imperial rulers. An aura of irony must have been present in the Trusteeship Council when the representative of the Soviet Union on several occasions made his moving pleas for self-government and human rights in the colonies.

— 4 —

PROBLEMS AND PROGRESS IN BRITISH AFRICA

British African Territories. In the part of Africa which is the subject of this study, Britain has responsibility for the following territories on the west coast: Gambia, Sierra Leone, the Gold Coast, and Nigeria, together with the trust territories of Togoland and the Cameroons. In East Africa the British territories are Kenya, Uganda, and the trust territory of Tanganyika, and in East Central Africa there are Northern Rhodesia and Nyasaland, which recently joined in a federation with the self-governing state of Southern Rhodesia. Far to the south, Britain is responsible for three protectorates with euphonious names Bechuanaland, Swaziland, and Basutoland. These will be discussed in the next chapter on the Union of South Africa.

In British West Africa, with its more than thirty million people, the Gold Coast and Nigeria have been the scenes of remarkable post-1945 developments in nationalism and self-government. With a population of four and a half million, the Gold Coast has enjoyed the

reputation of being the most prosperous and progressive
colony in Africa. Climate has ruled out white settlement,
Europeans cannot buy native land, and a rich agricultural
system is carried on by small peasant farms rather than
huge European-controlled plantations. The basis of Gold
Coast prosperity is cocoa production, which was only
40 tons in 1896 but in the 1950's reached the prodigious
figure of more than 300,000 tons. In addition, the colony
exports timber, gold, manganese, and diamonds.

Crown Colony Development. As a background to
understanding political developments in the British colonial empire since the war, a brief description of the governmental setup and the prevailing philosophy of native
rule before 1945 will be helpful. In all British colonies
the so-called *crown colony system* was in operation.
Every dependency was provided with a governor, assisted
by an executive council, and a legislative council. In the
latter, members, both officials and those from the unofficial community, might be nominated by the governor,
or the constitution could provide for the election of the
"unofficial" members. But no matter what the formula,
the governor always had sufficient votes from the official
members to carry through any legislation or desired
policy. This system had been in effect in the early days
of such British colonies as Natal, Cape Colony, the
Australasian colonies, and those in Canada. And by a
process of evolution, the official majority had been removed, self-government had been granted, and finally in
the last phase, the colonies had become completely sovereign nations. Implicit in the crown colony system, therefore, was the British objective of complete self-government
even in the non-European dependencies.

In British Africa hand in hand with crown colony
government went *indirect rule*. This system was used
where the traditional authority of the chiefs was strong,
or as in Northern Nigeria, where the local rulers—the
emirs—were figures of dignity and tradition. These chiefs
and emirs were permitted to continue their rule subject
to the over-all inspection of British officials. Indirect rule
endeavored to utilize the best elements in native society,
those the Africans respected and understood. It believed
that change should be gradual, that modern ideas should
gradually be grafted on to the framework of traditional

tribal government. In short, indirect rule aimed at being a school for self-government with the pupils the so-called native authorities. Underlying this system was the basic philosophy that the function of British rule was not to destroy the traditional culture and institutions of the African, but rather to conserve their positive elements, blending in whatever could be used with Western culture. Indirect rule was diametrically opposed to that system of native administration which ignored traditional chiefs and substituted in their place European officials. Known as *direct rule,* this was the type utilized by the Germans in East Africa and generally by the French in their tropical African possessions before World War II.

Postwar Unrest in the Gold Coast. In tracing the advance of self-government in the Gold Coast, the germs of nationalism began to ferment before the last war. In 1930, for example, Dr. Danquah formed the Gold Coast Youth's Conference, which was an association of young intellectuals interested in advancing their country. During the war the British Colonial Secretary visited the colony and was presented with a memorandum urging a consti- tutional advance. As a result, in 1946 a new constitu- tion was introduced. It superseded the system introduced in 1925 by which, for the first time, Africans could elect their representatives to the legislative council. The gov- ernor, however, had his official majority, which enabled him to carry any measure. A marked advance was made in 1946, when an unofficial majority was provided for —for the first time in any British African Colony. At the same time the membership of the executive council was modified to include three unofficial members. While this new Constitution was unprecedented in its advance of African responsibilities, it soon became evident that it did not go far enough to catch up with the mood of Gold Coast nationalism. As a British Report later ob- served, the 1946 constitution "was outmoded at birth." Following peace, the United Gold Coast Convention was formed in the summer of 1947 with the aim of achieving "self-government in our time." The following year wit- nessed serious disturbances. There was much unrest in the colony; a parade of ex-African servicemen got out of hand, forcing the police to fire. There were riots all over the dependency and some 250 were injured and 29

killed. The leaders of the United Gold Coast Convention
were imprisoned.

A special body known as the Watson Commission was
then appointed to investigate the colony's disturbances.
It found that the hopes of returned soldiers for "a golden
age for heroes" had been disappointed, that there was
deep political frustration among the educated classes,
and that there was strong suspicion of the government
everywhere. In addition, the traditional rule of the chiefs
was on the wane; the control of trade by foreigners,
especially the Syrians, and the cutting down of diseased
cocoa trees by agricultural officers were both resented.
Following this *Report* which advocated substantial political advances, a local body under the chairmanship of an
African judge—now Sir Henley Coussey—was appointed.
The Coussey Committee was all African—thirty-eight
members—and it made its recommendations in October
1949. This *Report* was hailed as a remarkable document,
one that marked a decisive turning point in African history.

Self-government for the Gold Coast. The new constitution that resulted set up a legislature that had jurisdiction over all the country: the colony proper, Ashanti,
and the Northern Territories. There were eighty-four lawmakers—seventy-five Africans and nine Europeans, three
of the latter being officials. These last three had charge
of the departments of Justice, Foreign Affairs, and
Finance, while the British governor had reserve powers
to enable him to veto or force through any measure.
Members of the legislature, eight Africans and the three
officials, also constituted a cabinet that could be dis-
missed by a two-thirds vote of the legislature. While the
traditional chiefs were represented in the legislature,
much of their power, and with it indirect rule, was done
away with by a new scheme of local government. New
ruling bodies called *councils* were set up. In them the
ruling chiefs, serving as the formal presidents, were only
figureheads. Two thirds of the membership of these
councils was elected by popular vote; the remainder was
selected from the traditional chiefs and elders. This substantial alteration of the old system of indirect rule was
an admission that the tribal authorities had not kept up
with the political aspirations of their people. This was

especially true in the Gold Coast. One British missionary on the West Coast observed that indirect rule was a "conception of genius" which had been allowed to "degenerate into a fetish." There was no doubt that the substantial modification of indirect rule would have repercussions throughout Africa. It meant that the so-called detribalized, Western-educated African, with his advanced notions of ballot-box democracy, was going to oust the old tribal authorities. In effect, the Gold Coast constitution brought the country to the verge of full self-government, with a cabinet no longer in an advisory capacity, but responsible for all acts of government except finance, justice, defense, and foreign affairs.

In these hectic days, as Africans all over the continent hailed the political progress made in the Gold Coast, a new leader appeared to direct his people to the promised land of freedom. Kwame Nkrumah, born on the edge of the Gold Coast jungle, had managed to attend missionary schools and finally graduated from Achimota College in 1931. Leaving the colony, the young man came to the United States and attended Lincoln University in Oxford, Pennsylvania (*See Reading No. 20.*) With his B.A. degree in his pocket he next journeyed to London University to study law. Legal treatises did not hold him long—the strong stimulant of the cause of African freedom soon possessed him. It was much more exciting, and then, too, Nkrumah began to earn recognition in London as an up-and-coming African nationalist. After the war he was called back home to be secretary-general of the new United Gold Coast Convention Party. As we have noted, in 1948 he was imprisoned following the outbreak of riots.

Victory for Nkrumah. Nkrumah did not long remain attached to the traditional leaders, such as Dr. Danquah, whom he regarded as old-fashioned. In June 1949 he founded his own party—the Convention People's Party—and began his campaign to secure mass support for his program. He denounced the Coussey Report and attempted to call a general strike to back up his demands. These tactics fizzling out, Nkrumah was again made His Majesty's guest in one of the prisons. But his plans had been well laid. In February 1951 elections were held for the new legislature. Nkrumah's C.P.P. carried out a campaign of mass propaganda. Its slogan was "Self-Government Now," leaving nothing else for other parties to stand for. The result was a thumping victory for Nkrumah, who was released by the governor and became the chief minister, the leader of government business, in the new legislature. Incidentally, this Gold Coast election provided for manhood and womanhood suffrage and was admirably arranged by the colonial officials. The public relations department trained special teams to tour the country, lecturing and showing movies explaining how the election would work. The majority of the voters being illiterate, special arrangements had to be made to assist them at the polls. No wonder the election has been described as the greatest single political development in the history of modern Africa.

The new constitution was soon modified (March 1952) to make Kwame Nkrumah prime minister of the Gold Coast. In 1954 came yet another advance. The legislature became all-African, the English officials giving up their portfolios of justice and finance. And the cabinet is also all-African, a responsible body like that in Westminster back in London. Only matters of defense and foreign affairs, together with the administration of the trust territory Togoland, remain reserved in the hands of the British governor. How soon Nkrumah and his colleagues would be satisfied with just less than full nationhood was a basic question in 1955. It was apparent, however, that if the Gold Coast Africans made a success of their new government, it could not be long before their country would have full dominion status and would be attending that exclusive club, the Imperial Conference of the Commonwealth.

One aspect of Nkrumah's program should be noted. His advisers drew up a new plan of development whose aim was "full employment and social security." Among its objectives were: (1) the modernization of agriculture, (2) the building of local industry, (3) the extending of road, railway, and air communications, and (4) the improvement of health and educational facilities. In the last-mentioned the aim is universal schooling on the elementary levels. In higher education the new University College at Achimota and the College of Arts, Science and Technology at Kumasi constitute notable advances.

It is hoped to finance the development program's cost of some £74,000,000 out of governmental revenue, with one third of the cost from loans. This does not include the tremendous undertaking known as the Volta River Project, which will have to be financed by foreign capital. The undertaking calls for the construction of a great dam capable of producing 500,000 kilowatts of power. This will be used to manufacture aluminium from the colony's vast deposits of bauxite.

Nigeria: Its People and Their Country. Leaving the Gold Coast and its dynamic leader, Prime Minister Nkrumah, we now take up the equally challenging developments in the largest political unit in Africa. This is Nigeria, covering an area of 370,000 square miles and with a population of some 28,000,000. One hundred miles inland from its Venice-like and overcrowded capital, Lagos, which is built on islands and extends to the mainland, is Nigeria's great city of Ibadan. This is the largest city in Africa between Cairo and Johannesburg. Nigeria, great as it is in size, is only a geographical expression; it is a conglomeration of diverse peoples, cultures, and creeds held together, heretofore, only by British rule. In the North are the aristocratic Fulani and the Hausa people; comprising more than half the total population, these Moslems are monarchist and conservative in tradition. Here proud and aristocratic emirs administer —subject to British advice—the affairs of emirates with populations of more than 2,000,000. These principalities have their own courts, police, treasuries, and schools. Under their system of indirect rule, British administrators have followed a policy of hands off, permitting the people to retain and utilize their own laws and customs. These Hausas and Fulani are proud of their culture and have shown little eagerness to take on the white man's culture. In the South are the two main ethnic groups, the Yorubas and the Ibos. The latter number 8,000,000, crowded on insufficient and rather poor land. In consequence, the Ibo are an expansionist and immigrant group who look upon all of Nigeria as their oyster. Unlike the Hausa to the north, they are eager to adopt Western culture; they have a zest for business, and a keen desire for education. The Yorubas living in the Southwest number some six and a half million. While not as restless and driving as the

Ibo, the Yoruba are an independent and gifted people. There are, of course, ethnic groups other than those we have mentioned; but these three—the Hausa, Yoruba, and Ibo—are the dominant peoples. While the first is mainly Moslem, the other two are pagan, Christian, and some Moslem, and a great religious chasm divides North and South.

In tracing the political history of Nigeria, it is best to begin with its amalgamation in 1914, when its disparate parts were united as the Colony and Protectorate of Nigeria. In 1922 a new constitution provided for a legislative council, which included the first elected Africans in any legislature in British Africa. This council in the main acted only for the colony and the western and eastern provinces in the South: it had little to do with the self-governing Moslem emirates in the North. During the 1920's and 1930's, there was some growth of nationalistic sentiment among the western-educated Nigerians in the South, but as in the Gold Coast, it was not until World War II and after that political aspirations mounted at incredible speed. In particular, the Atlantic Charter stirred the national hopes of young Nigerian patriots. In April 1943 the West African Students Union in London sent a demand to the Colonial Office asking for dominion status. A group of West African editors led by Dr. Azikiwe, who prepared a memorandum entitled *The Atlantic Charter and British West Africa,* visited Britain and asked for a substantial liberalization of crown colony government.

The Richards Constitution. As in the Gold Coast, after 1945 Nigerian political expectations were high— that is, in the South. There was also considerable labor trouble; parts of the Nigerian press were very anti-European. Realizing the strength of this unrest, the British governor, Sir Arthur Richards, framed a new constitution which was adopted in 1946. This official had three aims in mind: to promote the unity of Nigeria, at the same time to protect the diverse cultures and traditions of its people, and to advance the cause of self-government. One of the distinctive features of the new constitution was the creation of regional councils in Northern, Eastern, and Western Nigeria. Their purpose was to allow each distinctive area to discuss its own problems and yet to be linked with a central legislature for all of Nigeria. Here were the germs of a federal system of government. In these new bodies the traditional African chiefs, especially from the north, were strongly represented. For the first time in Nigerian history there was a majority of unofficial members in the central legislature; but the governor retained reserve powers which in the last analysis could override any opposition.

This so-called Richards Constitution was a marked advance towards full self-government. The governor in addressing its lawmakers made an eloquent plea for their support and understanding. (*See Reading No. 21.*) But the extreme nationalists were not satisfied. Mainly from the coast, they boycotted the new legislature. Leading this fight was Dr. Nnamdi Azikiwe, an American-educated Ibo Nigerian. Known as Zik, this capable leader, the son of a government clerk, had spent nine years in the United States getting an advanced education. Returning to the west coast, he practiced journalism in the Gold Coast and then set up the newspaper, *The West African Pilot,* in Nigeria. Gradually he created his own chain of some half-dozen newspapers. Dr. Azikiwe formed the new political party, the National Council of Nigeria and the Cameroons (the N.C.N.C.). In 1947 he went to London with a deputation demanding that the Richards Constitution be replaced by a more advanced one. While on this mission, Zik visited the United States, where he was warmly received, especially in Negro circles. Much attention was given to him in the press, in particular by *Time* magazine, which saluted him as "the Negro Gandhi," and the "jungle George Washington." Returning to Nigeria, Zik and his colleagues received a tumultuous welcome from his Southern supporters. In huge processions banners and placards were carried with such inscriptions as "Freedom or Death" and "Down with Imperialism." The press welcomed Zik and his heroes, and while regretting their failure in London, observed that "Nigeria has conquered Britain in a moral battle . . . fighting tooth and nail this monstrous spectre of cruelty and injustice—British imperialism." Zik's main political tenets were that the British had purposely kept Nigeria economically backward and that if the foreign interlopers would leave, the various peoples of Nigeria—

Ibos, Hausas, and others—would live happily together in a self-governing Nigerian nation.

The Constitution of 1952. To return to the system of government: It had been intended that the Richards Constitution should stand for nine years. In 1948, however, the new governor, Sir John Macpherson, urged the adoption of a new constitution. Put into operation in 1952, it gave the people of Nigeria semiresponsible government, bringing them to the verge of complete self-rule. The new system provided for increased regional autonomy in a Nigerian federation. The Moslem North successfully demanded half of the seats in the new legislature and the allocation of revenue on a per capita basis. In both this scheme of government and its predecessor of 1946, the suffrage had been given to all adult taxpayers, regardless of sex, except in the North, where women could not vote. As in the Gold Coast, and in new South Asian nations like India, this was a bold experiment in democracy without a literate electorate.

The constitution was launched with high expectations. It soon became apparent, however, that Zik had underestimated the divisive forces operating in Nigeria. There was not only keen rivalry between him and Mr. Awolowo's Yoruba party, the Action Group, but there was the greatest gully between both of these more or less Western-oriented parties and the people of the North. Educated Hausa leaders maintained that the Ibos assumed a pose of superiority over their people. They intensely disliked the crowding in of the Southerners, who with their new ways obtained jobs in the railways, telegraph, and other skilled employment. Furthermore, the Hausas did not like the zeal of the Ibos for party politics. And they had no liking for the new boom shantytowns of these pushing Southerners that were growing up outside the city limits of their towns. The breach was further widened when Zik demanded complete self-government by 1956. Answering this demand in the legislature, a Northern Moslem declared that if the British were now forced out his people would march and conquer to the sea. In reply a Southerner trumpeted: "I agree that if at this stage the European should quit this country, it would be inevitable that we immediately resume our tribal wars; but . . . much as it may be possible for the Northerners to attempt to overrun the South, so it is possible to take the Southerners no time to sweep across the Sahara desert." The Moslem North wanted self-government, but at a time and in a way that assured the integrity of their own way of life.

Regional Rivalries and Federation. In 1953 the smoldering feud burst into the ugly flame of violence. Serious riots broke out at Kano, a northern city, where the emir's government refused to allow the Southern Action Group to hold a public meeting. Rioting followed for three days, martial law was proclaimed, and 46 people were killed with 200 seriously injured. As the *Manchester Guardian* put it: "One thing is quite clear. This is a clash of Nigerians against Nigerians, not against the British." On May 21, a few days after the riots, the British Colonial Secretary announced that the constitution would have to be amended "to provide for greater Regional autonomy and for the removal of powers of intervention by the Centre in matters which could, without detriment to other Regions, be placed entirely within Regional competence." Conferences were held in both London and Lagos on the issue of amending the constitution. Tempers ran high and objectives seemed irreconcilable among the Nigerians, but finally agreement was obtained for a new system which, called the Federation of Nigeria, gave precise guarantees to the various regions against encroachments from the federal government. For the first time, the powers of government were divided between the regions and the center. Lagos becomes the new capital of the federation, which will retain sufficient power to maintain the territory's unity. Because of the divisive rivalries still present in Nigeria, the powers of self-government conferred by this constitution of 1954 do not go as far as those enjoyed in the Gold Coast. The governor general still has substantial powers in designated fields, such as defense, justice, the public services, and foreign affairs, and above all in the event of any emergency. In the main, however, the governor general will act in accordance with the advice of his African ministers.

As in the Gold Coast, African leaders in Nigeria are intent on economic development. Original plans drawn up at the end of the last war called for grants totalling $92,000,000 from the British Colonial Development and

Welfare Fund, together with local appropriations of
$120,000,000. These figures have subsequently been re-
vised and expanded. With economic advancement and
political unity, Nigeria has the makings of a great state
in the family of nations. But the matter of unity is imperative. If the various nations—for that is what they
are—do not learn to work harmoniously together both
for the progress of the whole country and yet at the same
time for the development of each area according to its
own genius and desires, partition of some sort will be the
unhappy result.

British East Africa. Turning from the interesting
story of the development of Black self-governing nations
in British West Africa, we now consider an area with
altogether different geographical features, and in consequence, distinctive problems and trends. This is British
East Africa, comprising the colony of Kenya, the protectorate of Uganda, and the trust territory under the United
Nations of Tanganyika. These three territories cover an
incredibly large area—642,000 square miles of land and
38,000 of water—with a population of about 18,000,000,
98.5% of whom are Africans. The nonnative people are
predominantly European and Asiatic, the latter from
India and what is now Pakistan. Europeans number
30,000 in Kenya, some 11,000 in Tanganyika, and 3,500
in Uganda; immigrants from India, together with some
Arabs, number about 225,000, the bulk of whom are in
Kenya.

East Africa is a fascinating land. It has nearly all
varieties of scenery, climate, and physical features. There
are great snow-capped mountains such as Kilimanjaro
and Mount Stanley, a hot and humid coastal plain, the
burning deserts of Kenya's northern province, and the
green lush plains of the European Highlands. The one
central fact about East Africa is its great elevated plateau
where altitudes vary from 5000 to 9000 feet and where
Europeans can live amid a pleasant moderate climate.
Many of the European settlers sleep under blankets every
night in farmhouses that are practically on the equator!
All this diversity lies in an area between the great lakes
of Central Africa and the Indian Ocean.

There are more than two hundred tribes in East Africa.
While the Bantu strain is dominant, there are tribes that

are Nilotic and Hamitic, and those that are mixtures in varying degrees of Hamitic and Bantu blood. The names of these tribes sound strange but musical: Swahili, Turkana, Baganda, Wanyakyusa, Chagga, and Kikuyu. Some of these people are pastoral herders of cattle who are warriors in tradition—such as the Masai—but the majority are farmers, like the Kikuyu who followed a primitive form of shifting cultivation (that is, the brush is burned off and the land cultivated until its natural fertility is exhausted and then the African moves on to new land). While not as rich in natural resources as the Gold Coast or the Belgian Congo, East Africa produces a wide variety of products, mainly agricultural, which in 1952 accounted for £120,000,000 in exports. Uganda is a large producer of coffee and cotton; Tanganyika has one of the most valuable diamond mines in the world, together with substantial exports of sisal and coffee, while Kenya produces the largest supply of pyrethrum in the world, as well as soda ash, dairy products, and wheat. All in all, as the author discovered, East Africa is a land of contrasts: of the beauty of coastal beaches studded with palms, of great mountains, and of stark deserts, above all; of prosperous and modern cities like Nairobi, capital of Kenya, with its 120,000 population living only a few miles from a great game reserve where lion, zebra, and giraffe roam unmolested. Contrast and diversity are evident in climate and scenery, but they are most important in the field of human relations. East Africa is a plural society where races of different cultures, varying traditions, and contrasting advancement are living. What group should be dominant—if any? What type of government should be the goal? Should the various races be kept apart or should the objective be the development of a harmonious, interracial society? These and other questions have agitated parts of East Africa for the past thirty years, mainly in Kenya and to some extent in Tanganyika. No wonder that a settler recently declared: "It is no exaggeration to say that next in importance to the problem of the relations between Russia and the rest of the world comes that of the color problem in [East] Africa today." [9]

[9] Cited in Olive Holmes, "Peoples, Politics and Peanuts in Eastern Africa," *Foreign Policy Reports* (December 1, 1950) p. 163.

Effective British occupation of East Africa goes back a scant fifty years. In the 1880's as we have seen, Germany and Britain first occupied and pegged out their claims. Their agents, however, were private trading companies. It was in 1888 that the British East Africa Company was formed; its agents did yeomen service in occupying Uganda and what is now Kenya. Insufficient funds, however, forced the company to dissolve, and the British Government, somewhat against its will, was forced to take over the administration of the two territories. In 1894, therefore, a protectorate was declared over Uganda and the following year over Kenya. Meanwhile the important decision had been made by the British to build a railroad from Mombasa on the Kenya coast to Uganda. This was a difficult engineering feat, for the grade started at sea level, climbed to more than 7000 feet, then descended to the Great Rift Valley, from which the railroad then climbed to 8500 feet before it finally gradually came to the shores of Lake Victoria at 5000 feet. This project cost five and a half million pounds, covered by the British taxpayer, but the railroad helped to open up Central Africa, protected the sources of the White Nile, and above all, started the experiment of the European Highlands.

Origin of Kenya White Settlement.   The first British administrators were delighted by the great stretches of fertile plateau enjoying a climate similar to a warm English summer. Laws were enacted in 1902 regulating the acquisition of land by European settlers. The following year English and South African immigrants began to arrive to take up land in the Highlands. At this time the greater part of the Kenya plateau was vacant or was used by the Masai for sporadic hunting ventures. There was no thought then that African and settler interests might clash. From the first the government began to set aside adequate lands, known as native reserves, for the various African tribes.

The pioneer of white settlement was Lord Delamere, who first visited Kenya, then the British East African Protectorate, on a shooting expedition in 1897. In 1903 he returned to settle and acquired large land holdings. At his famous Equator Ranch he began experimenting with various farm ventures, especially sheep and cattle raising.

Much of his personal fortune was spent in this agricultural pioneering, and he proved what could be done on the land of the Highlands. In 1912 he produced twenty bushels an acre on some of his plots; in Canada the average runs about twelve. European settlement grew slowly. The First World War, of course, halted any development as many Kenyans joined the fight against the German neighbors in nearby German East Africa. Following the conclusion of hostilities, settlement picked up again and in 1919 an ambitious ex-officer scheme of land development was launched. The postwar boom, however, was followed by a slump, and a number of farms were given up by discouraged newcomers. By the mid-twenties confidence had been fully restored and steady progress was being made in developing the colony's resources. Again, however, Kenya together with the rest of the world was buffeted by depression in 1930. Many farmers who had bought their land at fairly high prices—as had also been true in the United States—were now having difficulty paying their debts; their products were sold in a market where prices had collapsed. The discovery of gold in 1931 in somewhat limited quantity helped some of the settlers. By the late 1930's the colony had managed to stabilize itself economically. By this time the European settlement was 16,000, with a little more than 2,000 farms.

Controversy in Kenya. From the very beginning of white settlement Kenya had gained the reputation of being the bad boy in the British colonial empire. This dependency seemed to be a kind of colonial volcano, always working up steam for some controversy. The English settlers were no worse and no better than their American prototypes who came to the New World of the Americas. Serious problems were bound to develop by the mere fact of the existence of a capable and aggressive European community plumped down in the midst of a primitive collection of African tribes. From the beginning, the English settlers spoke of Kenya as a "white man's country." They demanded from the Government the right to elect their own representatives to the legislative council; in 1910 they organized their own association to bring pressure on the Colonial Office and to publicize their views.

From 1920 to 1939 there was almost continuous debate over various issues, not only in Kenya but in the British Parliament and by the general public. Debate revolved around the settler demand for self-government, the protection and adequacy of native lands, the conditions under which African labor should be secured, and whether the moneys obtained from native taxes were being spent for the African's benefit. Following the First World War, not only the European settlers but the Indian community demanded equal elective representation and on a common European-Indian voters roll. After tempers had risen high in both the Indian and settler communities, the British Government in 1923 issued its famous white paper, which ruled out not only the Indian demands but at the same time the possibility of European political dominance. In effect, the rights and the interests of the majority race, the Africans, must be "paramount."

Settler Discontent with Colonial Office Rule.   In the next few years controversial issues continued to emerge. The settlers accused the Colonial Office in London of being too partial to native interests. Liberal opinion in Britain continually criticized what was termed the exploitation of a helpless majority by the dominant Europeans. A number of important commissions were appointed to study various facets of the Kenya problem: the adequacy of native land, the operation of justice, the allocation of public funds to the various communities, the question of closer union—that is, administrative integration of Kenya —with the contiguous territories of Uganda and Tanganyika. The settler community was articulate, vehement, and at home in England had been accustomed to telling the M.P.'s in Parliament what they could or could not do. It was particularly galling for these well-educated Britons, who, after all, had sunk their fortunes in Kenya land, to be told that basic policy must be the responsibility of the Colonial Office and this department's master —Parliament. Crown colony government prevailed. The governor with his official majority could always block opposition to his measures or create his own opposition to block a settler measure frowned upon by the Colonial Office. On some occasions the settlers invoked the Spirit of 1776 and threatened to take over the government!

As in the case of other African colonies, the long

arm of World War II caught up Kenya. Many of its Europeans joined the armed services, or if they stayed in the Highlands, they worked hard and late producing the food so desperately needed. Thousands of Africans also did war duty, some of them as soldiers overseas. With the coming of peace the auguries appeared favorable for renewed Kenyan progress. A development plan was drawn up costing £41,000,000. Exports in 1952 amounted to more than £26,000,000 as compared with less than £4,000,000 in 1938.

The Mau Mau Crisis. But these hopes for tranquillity and development were tragically smashed by the advent of a sinister and horrible conspiracy that caused the deaths of hundreds of people—mainly Africans—and the dislocation of the colony's economic affairs. This crisis was caused by the secret, terroristic society known as the Mau Mau. The exact nature and the manner of its origin are obscure. (*See Reading No. 22.*) African unrest, especially among the Kikuyu tribe, is not new. For thirty years there has been evidence of various movements that were anti-European. The Mau Mau probably originated in 1948 and 1949, its leaders connected with the Kikuyu Central Association which was banned during the war. Also in the picture was the Kenya African Union whose President was Jomo Kenyatta. Educated in London, where he studied at the London School of Economics, and later in Moscow, the brilliant Kikuyu became intensely anti-European. From all accounts he was also personally most ambitious. His original aim was to use the nonviolent techniques of Gandhian passive resistance at the opportune time. The material for his movement was plentiful. While the Kikuyu tribe was more prosperous than it had ever been, it did have a serious and a growing shortage of land. Rumors were being spread that some of the land of their native reserve would be seized by the government. The Kikuyu were the nearest tribe to the fairly large city of Nairobi and to the largest concentration of Europeans. This proximity led to extensive detribalization. Kikuyu squatters worked on European farms, and thousands flocked into the city. Many, partially educated, semi-Westernized, and free from the old traditions and sanctions of the tribe, became

restless and disgruntled. Some of their number created
a vicious underworld in Nairobi and lived by murder
and theft.

Kikuyu Land Grievance. Agitators such as Kenyatta were able to exploit the deep grievance of the
Kikuyu about their land, a large area of which it is
claimed was taken by the White settlers. On the whole,
this charge was not justified, as the greater part of the
Highlands was never Kikuyu territory. Of the 6000 square
miles which can reasonably be said to be Kikuyu around
1906, only 106 were given to settlers. And for this loss
there was in the 1930's restitution of a cash payment
and the gift of land as a result of the recommendations
of the famous Carter Land Commission. Another way of
presenting this land issue is to point out that the European community, less than 1% of the population, has
20% of the best land in a country where there is much
desert and arid waste not suited to agriculture. To the
Kikuyu with their 6000 square miles supporting a million
people it is manifestly unfair for a farming community
of 15,000 to have 16,000 square miles (in reality only
12,000, since 4000 square miles is a forest reserve). The
issue, however, is not a simple one to be resolved by
comparing *quantity* of land; it would seem that *use* is a
significant factor. Produce sold off European farms, above
what was consumed on them, was worth £10,000,000 as
compared with the African production of £3,500,000.
Settlers point out that they contribute 70% of the colony's
total exports and pay more than twice as much as Africans
in direct taxes.

While this land problem is not a simple Black and
White issue, the leaders were able to take advantage of
the Kikuyu grievance. The rank and file in the Mau Mau
were apparently cowed and tricked into becoming the
dupes and blind followers of those in command. In ways
akin to the devilish technique of the police in totalitarian
Western states, the leaders gained control of the minds
of their masses. This was done by utilizing the old tribal
taboos and superstitions. Among the Kikuyu an oath is
a binding, even a terrible thing, not to be taken lightly.
The leaders, therefore, devised the *killing oath*. (*See
Reading No. 23.*) The most gruesome and orgiastic rites
were invented to capture the neophyte. In 1952 the Mau

Mau began their campaign of terrorism. On many a lonely farm, settlers were attacked and killed, betrayed by their servants who were unable to resist the command to kill. Africans who refused to join the Mau Mau, especially those who were Christians, were singled out for slaughter. In one terrible raid 150 Kikuyus, adults and children, were hacked to pieces.

Ending the Mau Mau Crisis. The Kenya government was apparently taken by surprise. But the police force was expanded, a sort of home guard of loyal Kikuyus trained, and more than 7000 troops brought in from Britain. At the end of 1954 nearly 7000 Mau Mau had been killed, while the casualties for the police and soldiers stood at 479, and tragically, 1300 civilians—Europeans and Africans—had been murdered. Fortunately, the Mau Mau movement affected only the Kikuyu; the other tribes remained loyal. By the end of 1955 the Mau Mau movement appeared to be on the verge of being crushed. Voluntary surrenders of Mau Mau became more frequent; only the fanatical elite remained at large skulking in the forest. Large numbers of Mau Mau, more than 83,000, were held in prison; many others were in temporary detention camps where they were being processed. While the rank and file will be released and moved to new locations, the bitter-enders will likely be settled in remote areas where they cannot cause trouble.

The net effect of the Mau Mau crisis has been to focus attention on Kenya anew and to force re-evaluation of the implications of its plural society. Before the war the concept of "white man's country" was strong. Today there are many settlers who realize that the best they can hope for is a multiracial society in which all elements have rights, safeguards, and opportunities. Among some Africans there is the extreme view that black African nationalism will prevail regardless of the interests of the immigrant communities. While the position of the European is being attacked, the status of the Indian community is also on the defensive. (*See Reading No. 24.*)

An indication of the growing recognition that some fundamental adjustments might have to be made in Kenya was given in the report of a British Parliamentary Delegation written in 1953. The members insisted that more outlet should be provided for African political am-

bitions, that the Africans should be encouraged to have
their own political associations, and that there should be
more progress towards the elimination of the color bar.
Most significant, the report, in stating that land should be
removed from the sphere of politics, hinted that there
should be some change in land policy. Another reflection
of change was the adoption of a new constitution in 1952,
which provided for a substantial proportion of African
members. Two years later a step was taken in the direction
of associating members of the legislature with the direction of executive policy. A new council of ministers was
set up on which six unofficials were represented: three
Europeans, two Asians, and one African. Only time can
tell whether a harmonious multiracial and democratic
society can be evolved in Kenya. This would have to be
one in which influence and weight would somehow be
equated between sheer numbers, level of civilization, and
extent of economic contributions.

Trends in Uganda and Tanganyika. Only the briefest mention can be made of developments in Uganda and
Tanganyika. As to the first territory, the British connection began in 1875 when H. M. Stanley visited the
country. A protectorate now with a population of just
under 5,000,000, there are only 4000 Europeans and an
Indian community of 37,500. Uganda is a more densely
populated and politically advanced country than Kenya
and more tropical in climate. European settlement never
gained headway. Nearly one third of the Africans live in
the kingdom of Buganda; the people are known as the
Baganda and speak a language called Luganda. The Baganda are a proud and capable people, one of the few
African tribes with a well-organized monarchical system
of government headed by a king—the Kabaka—and
with a parliament, the Great Lukiko. Since the last war
there has been considerable unrest; in 1949 and 1950
there were serious disturbances. In this mounting uneasi-
ness there was a confused blend of African nationalism,
suspicion of the immigrant races, and the separatist force
of old tribalism. In 1953 the youthful king of the Baganda asked for independence for his kingdom, which
heretofore had been joined with various other tribes and
with three important kingdoms in the Protectorate of
Uganda. This separatist action was inspired to some ex-

tent by Baganda tribal nationalism; but it also sprang from the rulers' fear of being some day joined with Kenya in a "closer union" project. The Kabaka also did not relish his country's being represented in a proposed all-Uganda legislature in which alien races—English and Indian—seemed to carry such disproportionate weight. Standing firm on his demands, the king was deported to England. This was in 1953. Negotiations were then carried on for two years, and in the fall of 1955 agreement was reached between the British Government and the Baganda leaders and their parliament. The Kabaka was to return; a new system of central government for all Uganda was agreed upon in which immigrant races will be represented but the basic interests of the kingdom of Buganda safeguarded. The separatist movement in Buganda had been blocked. Henceforth, this kingdom was to remain an integral part of Uganda. But while separatism may not reappear, in view of the growth of nationalism it is likely that African views and interests must come to prevail increasingly in the central legislature. This means that with so few Europeans and Indians, it is hard to believe that Uganda will develop into a truly multiracial state. Its destiny is that of a self-governing African state with adequate safeguards for the minority races.

Reference has already been made to Tanganyika in connection with the United Nations visiting mission's recommendation that this trust territory be prepared for full self-government in twenty years. This dependency has an African population of more than 7,000,000. Europeans number 11,000 and Indians 45,000. As in Kenya there is no doubt that the settlers and Indians have made —and will continue to make—important contributions to Tanganyikan progress. For this reason and because Britain naturally wants to see a continuance of her connection with this territory by means of White settlement, the government is striving to work toward a multiracial pattern in which the Africans will not be completely dominant. This means adequate safeguards for the Europeans and some political weighting in their favor as long as the great mass of natives are illiterate and primitive. One recognizes this as the same objective as in Kenya. At present, political representation is on the basis of political parity in the legislative council between Euro-

peans, Indians, and Africans. The United Nations visiting
commission in 1954, however, apparently had little use
for the multiracial principle. In the mind of the com-
missioners, self-government should be envisaged on a
purely democratic basis without respect to the rights of
racial minorities. The goal should be integration, the
removal of political parity, and the introduction of direct
elections. While there must be opportunity for full political growth on the part of the African, it is the view of
many competent observers that it is utterly unrealistic
to sweep away the safeguards of an advanced community
living among relatively backward peoples. For a considerable period the immigrant races have an important role
in the development of Tanganyika.

Federation in Central Africa. In British Central
Africa (to turn now to another area) the union of three
territories—Southern Rhodesia, Northern Rhodesia, and
Nyasaland—into a federation has been hailed as one of
the most important events in recent British colonial
history. This new state is officially the Federation of
Rhodesia and Nyasaland. It covers an area of 485,000
square miles, being larger than Texas, New York, and
California combined. On the whole it is sparsely settled,
with a population of 215,000 Europeans, 6,710,000 Africans, and 14,000 Asians. Southern Rhodesia has the
greatest bulk of Europeans and, with Northern Rhodesia,
was brought into the British Empire by the resolute and
aggressive expansionism of Cecil Rhodes. Early in the
1920's company rule established by Rhodes' efforts (The
British South Africa Company) ended. Southern Rhodesia
became self-governing in 1923, while Northern Rhodesia
passed under the control of the Colonial Office. The area
of the federation has rich natural resources, in minerals
and water power especially. Northern Rhodesia in 1953
produced £90,000,000 of copper. In addition, the three
territories marketed considerable quantities of tobacco,
lead, coal, cobalt, tea, cotton, cattle, and wheat. At the
same time, light industry is growing rapidly.

The Federation of Rhodesia and Nyasaland aims, first,
to raise the standards of living and expand governmental
services for the people of Central Africa. It is claimed
that only through this union can adequate capital be
raised, economic plans and development for all three

territories be envisaged, and the extensive resources of the area be adequately developed. In the second place, while the ultimate aim is self-government, the presence of a substantial British settler population tied in with the fortunes and policies of the three territories will mean a closer link with their homeland, Britain. This is not true in the case of the Negro self-governing Gold Coast. Third, this federation is another attempt to achieve a harmonious plural society. Some British statesmen consider the plan a roadblock against the extension from the south of the segregationist, White-domination policy of the Union of South Africa. A British periodical devoted to imperial affairs[10] has put the significance of this federation thus: "Is it or is it not possible for a multiracial community whose component parts differ not only in colour but also in stages of culture and civilization, in natural and acquired capacity, in tradition and custom, to be bound amicably together in a community which accepts the leadership of those best qualified to lead, and is content to work slowly towards an equal partnership which can only be based upon the real attainment of equality through a probationary and tutelary period of trust and goodwill?"

Pros and Cons of Federation. The federation of the Rhodesias with Nyasaland goes back at least twenty-five years. The question was discussed frequently, various conferences were held, and in 1939 a royal commission issued a report that dealt with the possibility of union. (*See Reading No. 25.*) During all this time the Africans in the two other territories have been opposed to any form of Closer Union with Southern Rhodesia. (*See Reading No. 26.*) After 1945 the issue was again raised. Important conferences were held, the first in London in March 1951. Despite opposition from Africans and a strong section of public opinion in Britain, the scheme of federation was carried through. This provides for a governor general representing the British Crown, a prime minister with a cabinet, and a federal assembly. Powers of government are divided between the central federal government and the three territorial governments. In order to allay African fears, an African Affairs Board

[10] *The Round Table* (London, June 1953) p. 228.

was set up to safeguard native interests. Any bill of the
assembly which it so designates is reserved for the approval of the British Imperial Government. Southern
Rhodesia is the dominant force in the Federation. And
while the native policy is not as liberal as some outside
critics would desire, it certainly is not in the same category
as that prevailing in South Africa. While there are more
than 47,000 European voters registered with only 320
Africans, it is important to remember that there is a
single voters' roll. Any person meeting the educational
and economic qualifications can get his name on this
voters' list regardless of race. Will "Equal rights for all
civilized men," a concept implicit in the single voters'
roll of Southern Rhodesia, evolve from a gesture to
reality? Will the present fears of the Africans gradually
be dispelled? Or will the native policy of the Federation
gradually move in the direction of that prevailing in South
Africa? These are the questions to be answered in the
next decade or so.

— 5 —

THE DIVIDED UNION: SOUTH AFRICA

Diverse and Beautiful South Africa.   The Union of South
Africa, though a member of the Commonwealth of
which Great Britain is the senior partner, is not an
integral part of that British Africa which we have just
discussed. For the Union is fully a sovereign state, and is
in the last instance ruled by its Afrikaner population,
who are mainly Dutch in distant origin and who have no
love for Britain and her works. South Africa is a land
of magnificent distances, being one sixth the size of the

United States. This country always charms the visitor who for the first time experiences its great diversity and beauty. Landing at Cape Town, one is awed by the magnificent prospect of Table Mountain, and motoring along the nearby coastal roads, is entranced by the beauties of the rugged coastline. In the province of Natal the visitor sees semitropical beaches backed by a green and lush terraced hinterland. Or traveling to Johannesburg one enters the most modern city in all Africa, now nearing one million inhabitants, with its skyscrapers dominating the skyline challenged outside the city only by the huge mountains of refuse dumps built by the mines. Back from the coast and set off by the great Drakensberg chain of mountains is the vast plateau of the veld, 4000 to 6000 feet in altitude. And everywhere, one feels the diversity of the people who live in this pleasant and temperate land: Europeans—Afrikaans—and English-speaking, East Indians—Moslems and Hindus—and a wide variety of Africans—Hottentots, Zulus, Basuto, Swazi, and Venda. The racial composition of South Africa's people is one of the most mixed and complicated in the world. Of the Union's 13 million, 2.75 million are Europeans, and of these about 1 million are English and 1.5 million of Dutch Boer descent, now known as Afrikaners. There are 10.5 million non-Europeans: of these 8.75 million are Bantus, 1 million are of mixed blood called Cape Colored, and 385,000 are East Indians. Of the entire population the Europeans constitute only 21%. These figures explain the deep concern of all Europeans lest they and their civilization be absorbed by the huge Bantu majority.

During World War I, South Africa was loyal to Britain, despite a small rebellion. Her leaders, Botha and Smuts, played an important role in the fashioning of victory and also at the making of the peace in Paris. Worn out with his labors, Botha, the apostle of good will between Boer and Briton, died in August 1919. During the rebellion of his own Boer extremists, Botha had pleaded with his people to forgive and forget. He had said: "Let us spare one another's feelings! Remember, we have to live together in this land long after the war is ended."

The Boer Nationalist Party. But little was forgotten by the extreme Boer nationalist faction. Smuts, who became prime minister, was reviled for his support of the British Commonwealth, for his internationalism, and for his rough tactics against unruly strikers in the gold mines. Postwar dislocations were difficult to handle; Smuts was blamed for all that took place. The result was his defeat at the polls in 1924 by General Hertzog, an ex-Boer general who had organized his own Nationalist Party in 1912. The election was won by an alliance between the backveld, i.e., the farmer or rural Boers, and the European trade-unions. Hertzog was primarily interested in making his Afrikaans' community every whit equal in status with the English element in South Africa and in having the Union recognized as an autonomous state. Afrikaans, a dialect derived from the old Dutch, was made an official language along with English and Dutch. More Afrikaners entered the government service, and steps were taken to give the Union its own distinctive flag and national anthem. Finally, Hertzog in the 1926 declaration of the Imperial Conference in London secured the recognition of South Africa as a sovereign state "equal in status" to the other members of the Commonwealth. In 1931 this concept was given legal form in the Statute of Westminster.

In the national election of 1929 the Nationalist Party whipped up White racialism on the slogan of "South Africa a White Man's Country." Again Hertzog led the government. But his regime soon was hit by world depression. The prime minister refused to go off gold and devalue currency as other nations had done. The effect was ruinous. At this juncture Smuts played the patriot. Refusing to take advantage, he offered to join Hertzog in a fusion government as deputy prime minister if Hertzog would abandon the gold standard. This was in 1934, and in a short time economic confidence was restored.

The Problem of a Multiracial State. The United Party, as this fusion was called, enacted some significant native legislation. By this time the problems of a multiracial state were becoming evident. The African natives far outnumbered the Europeans, and while the latter increasingly depended upon black labor, they had no intention of sharing power with the Africans, most of whom were illiterate and in the tribal stage. The pattern of native policy had begun to take shape as early as 1910 when the Union first began to function. Non-Europeans were not permitted to sit in the Union parliament, although they could be members of the Cape Provincial Council. The old Boer principle applied to the natives of "No equality in Church and State" was continued in the Transvaal and Free State. It was also maintained in a "decently clothed" form in Natal. Only in the Cape, with its liberal English tradition, was a common voting roll for all, with property and literacy, retained. The pattern of segregation between the races also took form. Native lands or reserves were definitely demarcated in 1913, and no native could own land outside of these areas. In 1923 the segregation of natives in urban areas or locations was also provided for. At the same time, with little official legislation, the color bar was applied in industry to lock the door of skilled work to the African. As part of the machinery of keeping the natives under control in the White areas, a pass system was devised that required the African to show that he had been allowed to leave his reserve, additional documents had to be carried showing the nature of employment and place of residence; in addition a special night pass must be carried after curfew hours. These passes, ordinarily, have not been required in the Cape Province; but they are required elsewhere and have led to much bitterness between the natives and the police who enforce the requirement.

In the middle 1930's several important acts were passed for the purpose of tightening up and systematizing native policy. The native reserves were recognized as inadequate. Additional land was to be purchased by the government; and when the full amount was added, the reserves would occupy 58,000 square miles, or 13% of the area of the Union. (In 1955 land had been added to bring the percentage to 9.7.) An act deprived Africans in the Cape from voting on the common roll. They were given the right to vote separately to elect three Europeans to the Union House of Assembly and two Europeans to the State Provincial Council. At the same time South African natives were given the opportunity of electing four Europeans to the Union Senate. Thus the last remnant of direct participation by Africans in elections had

been expunged. A Natives' Representative Council for
the entire country was set up, in which Africans were
strongly represented, but their function was purely advisory. While African political rights were being whittled
away, those of the Europeans were being expanded. In
1930 all European women were granted the vote; the
following year, without any qualification, all men were
enfranchised. Smuts had a somewhat more liberal view
on native policy than did Hertzog. While believing in
White Supremacy, he was willing to make compromises
and was cognizant of the fact that the Africans were
human beings with pride and sensitivity. In the long run
Smuts hoped that the native would be allowed to advance
in a structure of gradually decreasing separation. While
some of the above-mentioned laws did not please him,
Smuts nevertheless cooperated with Hertzog to try to
reduce tension.

Dr. Malan, Ultra-Boer Nationalist.   Tranquillity, like
English sunshine, is not an enduring phenomenon in
South Africa. Disgusted by the alliance between Hertzog
and the "pro-British" Smuts, Dr. Daniel Malan took up
his cudgels and established a new Nationalist Party. From
1936 to 1938 much bickering went on between the British
and Afrikaner elements over the language question, the
national flag, the uniform for South African sailors, and
so on. Another explosive issue was that of the transfer
of the protectorates. At the time of the Union, in 1909,
the three native states of Basutoland, Swaziland, and
Bechuanaland, all geographically part of South Africa
were not included. (*See Reading No. 27.*) Their African
people opposed coming under the new government. In
the 1930's the South African Government formally raised
the issue of transfer. As the inhabitants of the protectorates were by this time more disinclined than ever to come
under native policy dominated by the Afrikaner, and as
liberal opinion in England strongly opposed giving up
the protection of these protectorate natives, the British
Government refused to accept any change in their status.
The issue, however, lay dormant and Nationalist leaders
did not give up their claim to these native territories.

The rise of Hitler also exacerbated the situation. Here
was a leader who really stood for something—so it appeared to an influential circle of Afrikaners. They ap-

proved of Hitler's race theories, they enjoyed his snubbing of Britain, and they liked his political authoritarianism. As the threat of war loomed, there were many pro-Nazis in the Union. War finally came and on the issue of neutrality or belligerency, Smuts displaced Hertzog and joined Britain. This action split the United Party; many of its Afrikaans members joined Malan. Hertzog passed into political oblivion and from the South African scene entirely by his death in 1942.

During the war Smuts was a great leader, giving Britain and his friend Churchill staunch support. He reached his full stature as soldier, statesman, scientist, and philosopher. His life is worthy to be studied as a chronicle of versatility in mental achievement and bold leadership in character. One of his last contributions was the writing of the preamble to the Charter of the United Nations. The tide of nationalism in South Africa, however, had strengthened after 1945, and Smuts' followers lacked the uncompromising zeal of the Nationalists following Malan. The result was defeat for Smuts in 1948. Two years later, at the age of eighty, Field Marshal Smuts passed from the scene where he had for so long made history. With his passing many Nationalists felt that a new epoch had begun: "At last we have got our country back." As for the English and for those Afrikaners who had been in the United Party working for the future rather than the past, they keenly felt the loss of their leader. And tragically, Smuts' deputy prime minister and presumed heir, the brilliant liberal-minded Jan H. Hofmeyr, had died in December 1948.

Apartheid in Action. Prime Minister Malan lost no time in putting the Nationalist policy on the statute books. (*See Reading No. 28.*) While personally he favored breaking the ties with the Commonwealth, on this matter he preferred waiting to know the sentiments of English South Africans. His main interest, therefore, was native policy. The Nationalist objective was known as *apartheid* (separateness). This has been succinctly defined as "social, economic, political, and sexual segregation on the basis of race." There are several concepts of *apartheid*. One stands for complete separation of the races: the removal of natives back to the reserves and the end of dependence of Europeans upon African labor.

Such *apartheid* would involve tremendous economic sacrifices on the part of the Europeans and is not in the realm of practical politics. The one that is operating is really *apartness with intermingling*. It involves the specific definition of the political, social, and economic status of the several racial groups constituting a multiracial society. In effect, it means utilizing Black labor in urban areas but keeping the Africans segregated socially, inarticulate politically, and second-grade artisans economically.

An amazing amount of legislation has come out of the Nationalist legislative hopper. To maintain race purity there are the Immorality Amendment Act, the Prohibition of Mixed Marriages Act, and the Population Registration Act. The first two are designed to prevent marriage between the races and any promiscuity. The third gives every citizen his "right racial label." This has been rather vulgarly referred to as the "National Stud Register."

The Group Areas Act seeks to ensure residential segregation. It sets aside definite areas for the exclusive occupancy of various races. This act has not yet been implemented because of the many difficulties of moving Africans from one area and obtaining housing for them in another, the matter of compensation, the question of land values, etc. The program, however, is now under way; in Johannesburg alone more than 50,000 Africans are to be moved. Other *apartheid* legislation affects education, African labor, and political rights. Schools for Africans, in the past largely in the hands of the missions, are now to be either sold or rented to the state. If the missions choose to continue to operate independently they do so with a greatly reduced government subsidy, making their operation very difficult. Under government control the aim of Bantu education is to prepare Africans for life "in accord with the policy of the state." Legislation in the field of labor reaffirms the fact that African unions do not possess legal recognition and gives the labor minister far-reaching powers to determine what occupations members of any race may follow.

Apartheid affected not only the African, but also the Indian community. Originally brought over in the 1860's as indentured workers to be employed on the sugar plantations, Indians were soon regarded as an undesirable and unassimilable element. Various kinds of repressive acts

were passed at the end of the nineteenth century imposing special taxes, restricting travel, segregating areas of
residence, and laying down barriers to certain occupations.
It was this situation that transformed Gandhi from a
professional lawyer in the Union to a self-denying reformer. Here he first brought the attention of the world
to the plight of the Indians and perfected his weapon
of *satyagraha,* or soul force with passive disobedience,
against the government. Some improvement was secured
but the controversy continued into the 1920's and 1930's.
After World War II the Indians were brought under the
Group Areas Act and other restrictive legislation affecting
them came into force. These actions aroused the sensitive
and proud, newly independent nations of Pakistan and
India. These states on several occasions have brought the
question before the United Nations and registered protests with the South African Government.

In the field of politics the aim of Malan's government
was to remove the last non-Europeans from the common
voting roll. The Separate Representation of Voters Bill
was aimed at the Cape Colored community—a mixed race
that thought of itself as more European than African.
The bill placed this community on a separate roll electing
four Europeans to parliament. It was passed by a simple
majority after a bitter debate in which the United Party
charged the bill with being unconstitutional unless passed
by a two-thirds vote. This was in accordance with the
constitution of 1909. On this entire *apartheid* program,
followers of Malan gave a spirited and confident defense.
(*See Reading No. 29.*)

Opposition to the Malan Program. The reaction to
the passage of the measure was the declaration by the
appellate division of the Supreme Court that it was unconstitutional. Malan then proceeded to pass another
measure which made parliament acting as a judicial body
superior to the Union's highest court. This again was
declared unconstitutional. Meanwhile the country was
stirred up as never before. Organizations, such as the
war veterans' Torch Commando, held mass meetings pro-
testing against the government's flaunting the constitution. The mounting tension led the United Nations to
appoint, late in 1952, a commission to study the racial
conditions. (*See Reading No. 30.*) Its 372 page report

is one of the most objective and informative surveys of the Union. (*See Reading No. 31.*)

The *apartheid* program had also brought the African population to the point of open defiance of law. For a number of years unsatisfactory living conditions and the operation of the pass laws had led to bitter resentment and lawlessness on the part of the urbanized natives. The *tsotsi*, black gangs of lawless young Africans, terrorized both Europeans and their own people. The police and the natives were continually carrying on hostilities; crime rose at an alarming rate. All of this involved violence, but the more responsible elements in urban African society also challenged the Government's actions in a dignified and restrained manner. Joined by the Indian community the African National Congress in 1952 called a passive resistance campaign against what were termed "unjust laws." More than 10,000 Africans were sent to prison for intentionally breaking various laws. While this defiance campaign was not successful, it failed because of lack of funds and because of the heavy penalties imposed by the authorities. Europeans in general, however, where surprised at the restraint and discipline exhibited by the Africans. Determined to crush any resistance, the Nationalist Government strengthened its coercive powers. The minister of justice was given the power to declare a state of emergency at his discretion and by the Suppression of Communism Act of 1950, amended in 1951, anyone can be convicted of subversive Communism who disobeys the law or even openly criticizes the existing order supported by the Nationalists.

Strijdom Provokes Crisis.   At the end of 1954 Dr. Malan was succeeded as prime minister by J. G. Strijdom. The new leader was more intransigent, more rigid on racial matters than his predecessor. One of the reasons was that his Nationalist Party had won the crucial national election in 1953. Because of the overrepresentation of rural areas, the Nationalists had won with a minority vote. Strijdom's slogan was *baaskap,* White supremacy. According to the new leader: "The white man will only succeed in remaining in South Africa if there is discrimination, in other words, only if we retain all power in our hands." In order to sweep away the safeguards provided by the constitution and to give one political party the power to change the governmental structure at will, laws were passed to ensure the supremacy of parliament. By increasing the members of the senate and altering the method of election, anti-Nationalist representation would be all but wiped out in all provinces except Natal. Another act sought to increase, or pack, the appellate court, ensuring a pro-Nationalist bench. These measures, becoming law in the summer of 1955, aroused wide opposition. Many influential scholars from the universities drew up protests, huge mass meetings were held, and a European women's organization carries on continuous picketing of the capital building with the placards, "Honor Our Constitution."

This, then, is the unhappy situation in the divided Union. It is not only Black versus White, but tragically the Europeans are a house divided against itself. No one can foretell the future, but it looks ominous. Expert opinion, even from the Nationalist camp, holds that pure *apartheid,* total separation, is impossible. Further, there is strong evidence to show that "practical *apartheid,*" that is, having some natives live in segregated areas outside the reserves working for Europeans, is in the long run impractical. The inexorable force of economics, in this case industrialization, is drawing the natives from their reserves. More and more, industry depends upon African labor, and without it the economy would collapse. Between 1921 and 1951 the urban native population increased 230%. Since 1939 the number employed in industry, all races, has more than doubled. At present more than 60% of the Bantu are outside the reserves. Even if they could be moved back to them, the land would not be sufficient to support the increased population. And if the economic structure with its new mines, power stations, and factories demands even more African labor than at present, it is apparent that this urbanization will continue to break down the old tribal ways. Contact with European life will strengthen the desire of the natives for more voice in his future. Sooner or later mass action, peaceful or violent, will become a possibility. Despite its modern weapons, it is difficult to see how 20% of the population can keep down the other 80%. Surveying this dismal prospect, there are some who have little faith in the future of the white race in South Africa. They not only see the teeming millions of Africans but also, across the Indian Ocean, those of Asia. One such observer, discussing *apartheid*, writes: "In the end, it would make no difference. Talk is useless. Africa is the black man's continent; it may also be the yellow man's continent. In Africa the white man is 'a transient and embarrassed phantom.'" [11] This well may be ultimately true, but there still remain South Africans who believe there is yet time—but very little—to work out a pattern of living ensuring opportunities for advancement on the part of the African with suitable safeguards for the European, as long as the great majority of the population are backward and at least partially primitive. Specifically, this might mean removal of the color bar in economics and politics; a man's vote and occupation regardless of race would depend on his ability and education. While social segregation might be retained, educated Africans in business and government would find opportunities for their talents. There would seem to be a much better chance for civilization in South Africa if all men who attain a civilized status are given the opportunity to enjoy and enrich it, rather than a minority trying to defend it by sheer force against both primitive Africans and those who have taken on advanced Western habits and values.

[11] Sarah G. Millin, "Smuts At Eighty," *Foreign Affairs,* October 1950, p. 142.

THE FRENCH, BELGIANS, AND PORTUGUESE IN AFRICA

ALTHOUGH British Africa, including the Union, over-shadows the rest of Africa—in population, over-all economic output, and degree of leadership, not to speak of its rapid political advancement and the acuteness of its racial problems—we now turn to a great African colony where there are no Mau Mau, where the Bantu do not glower at their white overlords, and where tranquillity reigns. As a Belgian authority has observed: "The Belgian Congo today is prosperous and peaceful. It shines by comparison with most African countries."

The Belgian Congo. This "tropical cornucopia," as it has been called, is an immense territory. Roughly one third the size of the United States, it would stretch, south to north, from the American shore on the Gulf of Mexico to the Canadian border. Eighty times the size of Belgium, this colony is relatively sparsely populated with only 12,000,000 Africans and 80,000 Europeans. Attached to the Belgian Congo is the trust territory of Ruanda-Urundi with a population of nearly 4,000,000, formerly part of German East Africa and administered under the United Nations.

Visitors to the Congo four or five years after World War II, after an absence of ten years, could hardly understand the degree of transformation that had taken place in such a short time. Great cities like Léopoldville and Elisabethville have been built, with modern office buildings, skyscrapers, and broad ribbons of automobile highways. And great industrial establishments, mainly mines, produce the most valuable and strategic minerals, such as uranium, in the world. In 1953 the Belgian Congo exported over $400,000,000 worth of goods, and its gross national product was more than a billion dollars. It produces half of the world's uranium and 70% of its industrial diamonds. Other minerals produced in substantial amounts are copper, cobalt, zinc, manganese, gold, and tungsten. In addition, it produces yearly $40,000,000 of cotton, $32,000,000 of coffee, and $28,000,000 of palm oil.

America's Ties with the Congo. A feature of this incredible industrialization has been the growing economic ties between the United States and the Congo. We now take 13% of its output, not including our purchases of uranium for our defense industry, which is a classified secret. In turn, 24% of all the colony's imports come from the United States. We now realize the immense importance of having access to the natural resources of the Congo. During the last war, when the Japanese overran South Asia and shut off supplies of rubber and tin, it was this area that furnished much-needed supplies of these and other commodities.

From the earliest Belgian contact with the Congo, great monopolistic enterprises have been given exclusive rights to develop the territory's natural resources. As we recall, the first activities of these corporations were tragic because of their callous utilization of African labor to produce tropical products, mainly rubber. But after 1908, when the Belgian Government took over the dependency from Leopold II's uncleanly grasp, these great industrial concerns have been carefully regulated so that the interests of the Bantu population would not be harmed. At the present time five great corporations control 90% of the Congo's capital investment. The biggest of these is the Société Générale. The Union Minière de Haute Katanga has a concession of 13,000 square miles —bigger than all Belgium—constituting the most valuable mining land in Africa. Another important corporation, with leases over two million acres, is controlled by the famous English soap company, Lever Brothers. In most cases the Government controls large blocks of the capital of these concerns, in some cases more than 50%.

Belgian colonial rule and the philosophy on which it is based is quite different than that prevailing in British Africa and in the Union of South Africa—and as we will shortly see, from that in the French and Portuguese colonies. Someone has said that the Belgians have no colonial policy if by this is meant a definite program of objectives, especially in the political field, as is the case with Britain and France. A Belgian authority on colonial problems has said: "Belgians do not burden themselves with prejudices and preconceived notions. Deprived of colonial traditions and thus deprived of all experience in this field, Belgium knows no reason, sentimental, historical, or political, why she should choose one colonial system rather than another." [12] The Belgians have never been interested in the ultimate aims of colonial rule. Perhaps the most pragmatic of colonial administrators, they have concentrated on one objective: the material advancement of the Congo and with it the raising of the native welfare of its indigenous inhabitants. (*See Reading No. 32.*)

Accent on Native Welfare. While concentrating on native welfare, little thought or effort is given to political training of the natives in the art of self-government. An African can go as far as his talents allow in the economic field, but he can hardly take one step in the political arena. In fact there are no politics, no voting, for Black or White in the Congo. One of its governors general has admitted that some form of self-government might evolve in a hundred years. In this efficient paternal regime, all directives and ultimate policy come from Belgium. Here colonial affairs are mainly in the hands of the minister of colonies advised by a colonial council that must be consulted on all matters. The colony is administered by a governor general assisted by a government council, but this body is purely consultative. A special feature of the Congo system is a Commission for the Protection of Natives whose function it is to check on any abuses of natives. All in all some 5000 Belgian officials do the ruling.

While there is no ballot for the relatively few Europeans and the twelve million Bantu, there is economic freedom and advancement for all. Native welfare is the key of Belgian colonial policy. It is claimed that the African is better housed and clothed in the Congo than anywhere else in Africa. Infant mortality, because of numerous health centers, is lower than that in Italy; 40% of the school population are in school—about one million

[12] Louis Kraft, "Rival Colonial Policies in Africa," *The Listener* (London, July 1, 1954) p. 13.

children; and in the cities slums are being torn down
for the erection of numerous housing projects for African
workers. In many urban areas the natives are being helped
to build their own homes. Modern facilities, clubs,
schools, and athletic fields are being provided by the great
corporations for their workers. Instead of the mine com-
pounds of South Africa, where men live segregated from
their homes and families, the large industrial concerns in
the Congo are providing housing for native families.

Congo Ten-Year Plan. One of the most significant
aspects of native welfare in the Congo is its ten-year
plan. This amazing program of social and economic development calls for the expenditure of one billion dollars,
nearly half of which has been already spent. The program
calls for many new government buildings and new housing for public employees. It expands hydroelectric plants,
railroads, and schools. Nearly a hundred million dollars
is to be spent on native housing alone. New hospitals
and health centers are to be erected and research of all
kinds subsidized. As part of this plan a new university
has been opened known as Luvinium, ten miles out of
Léopoldville; another is being opened at Elisabethville.

All this is not to say that the Belgian Congo is without its problems. Detribalization is taking place rapidly
as thousands of Africans stream into the cities. In 1938
a little over 8% of the natives were out of the tribal
areas, working in the mines and living in the cities. In
1954 the figure was 22%, amounting to more than two
and a half million natives. With this rapid urbanization
and the breaking down of tribal custom and law have
come numerous problems. Prostitution and vice are serious in some cities. The increasing African middle class
is growing restless. The government has given special
credentials to the relatively few Africans who can claim
to be truly Westernized. This recognition entitles the
évolué or the *immatriculés,* as these advanced natives are
called, to enjoy some of the legal and other rights possessed by the European population.

Careful attention is paid to White settlement, which
the Government has striven to keep to reasonable proportions; it is now only 80,000. The existence of the two
races creates problems revolving around the color-bar
question. It may be said that there have never been any

economic bars, but there are definite ones in social and personal relations. The Government, however, seems to be moving toward the reduction of segregation. In 1952 African children, duly qualified, were admitted to European schools, and transportation companies were advised to allow Africans to travel first-class if they could pay the fare.

A native policy which is creating a class of skilled African artisans earning $150 a month and which has seen native purchasing power rise six times in ten years certainly has something to be said for it. The accent is on material welfare, not politics. At the present time there is apparently little desire in the Belgian Congo for self-government. Perhaps times will change, but in 1955 the colony was quite tranquil under the official policy expressed as "We dominate in order to serve."

French Africa. On the map the possessions of France south of the Sahara overshadow those of Britain, for *Afrique Occidentale Française* (French West Africa) is an enormous territory of 1,850,000 square miles, and French Equatorial Africa is nearly 1,000,000 square miles in area. The former extends from Dakar to Lake Chad and from the Sahara to the Gulf of Guinea, being more than 2000 miles from east to west and slightly more than 1500 miles from north to south. French West Africa has a population of 18,000,000 Africans living in an area one sixth the size of all Africa. But one third of the territory is desert or semiarid, with a sparse population. Valuable crops are produced, but the area has few known minerals and the total wealth produced is nothing like that coming from colonies like Nigeria and the Gold Coast. As to Equatorial Africa, huge as was its size, the French neglected this colony woefully before World War II. While there are huge stretches of desert, there are also immense areas of rich and well-watered land waiting development. Before 1939 only 215 kilometers of railway had been built, the government budgets were small, and natural resources were not utilized. Generally speaking, in Africa the main emphasis of the French in developing their territories was on North Africa (Morocco, Algeria, Tunisia) which was more valuable than all the rest of the empire.

French Colonial Assimilation. Unlike the Belgians

and the British, the French had developed before 1939 a precise and logical theory of colonial rule. This theory is described as *assimilation*. The ultimate objective of French rule was not, as in the British colonies, to develop representative institutions by which self-government would be enjoyed in a rather loose relationship with the mother country. The aim, rather, was to integrate the overseas possessions with France, to assimilate the colonial people into the body of French political, social, and cultural thought and practice. In keeping with this philosophy, African languages and culture were given no place in French colonial education. The purpose was to make Frenchmen out of Africans, an aim thoughtfully described by the colonial specialist, W. B. Mumford, in his book *Africans Learn to Be French*. The unity of France and her overseas possessions in a *bloc français* not only stemmed from economic and political considerations but also from the faith of the French in their superior culture, "because every Frenchman believes in the universal mission and validity of French culture as France's greatest gift to the world." In short, the vision of France was a single bloc of territory inhabited by men of different color and on occasion of different religion, but men who regardless of their residence in Paris or Dakar were French in language and in culture, and who would all be represented in the parliament in Paris.

This was the ideal. How did it work out in practice? There were undoubtedly some excellent results. Peace, public works, new economic forces, and good but limited educational opportunities were given to the African colonies. In France educated and Westernized Africans were treated as equals and a few Africans attained high office, either in the French parliament or in the colonial service. But there were serious weaknesses. While the original French aim had been assimilation, it was realized in the closing years of the nineteenth century that the process of absorbing millions of primitive Africans would be long and difficult. Hence assimilation was tempered somewhat by what was referred to as *association*. By this was meant the education of a small group of Africans, an elite, that would be associated with the French officials in bringing Western culture to the masses. In the years before 1939, however, it was apparent that the elite was a very minuscule group, and further, that very few of these had been able to attain citizenship. In the political structure of French West and of Equatorial Africa there were a number of councils of only consultative power, and administration was dominated by Frenchmen. In the field of economics too, restriction rather than freedom prevailed. The colonies were either neglected or exploited for French benefit. Industries were discouraged and tariffs brought the colonies behind monopolistic walls.

As we have already seen in our discussion of World War II, this conflict strengthened the forces of reform in all the African Empires, the French included. By 1943 the reactionary Vichy government was eliminated in Africa and the destiny of the colonies was in the hands of the French Committee of National Liberation. A new look in colonial policy was definitely inaugurated at the Brazzaville Conference, held in February 1944. Its keynote was the creation of representative assemblies in the colonies, the establishment of a new colonial parliament in Paris, and extensive social and economic reforms. Note, however, that it was specifically stated that all this emphasis upon reform "dispels any idea of autonomy" or any "possibility of evolution outside the French imperial bloc." The basic ideal was still assimilation.

The French Union. The new colonial program envisaged at Brazzaville was given legal expression in the new constitution of the Fourth French Republic. This document was put into force in 1946. In its preamble and in Articles 60 to 81 the basic philosophy and the structure of the French Union are laid down. (*See Reading No. 33.*) The new political structure united France and her possessions in an indissoluble union. In brief, the overseas departments, territories, and states were given representation not only in the French parliament but in the Assembly of the Union, where half of the members were from overseas and the remainder from France. This French Union constitutes, at least at the present time, an illogical blend of old assimilation and new devolution. The Assembly of the Union in Paris strives to maintain the old idea of centralization, but the new colonial assemblies overseas are a step in the direc-

tion of local autonomy. In French West Africa there are
eight local assemblies which in turn send representatives
to the federal assembly in Dakar. In Equatorial Africa
there are four local assemblies which in turn send members to its federal assembly. All subjects in these two
colonies are now French citizens, and the electorate has
in consequence been enormously expanded. In 1951 there
were three million eligible voters in West Africa and in
the elections of this year about half of them went to the
polls. While nationalism and political discontent have not
evidenced themselves in French Africa—south of the
Sahara—there is evidence that educated Africans want
their territorial assemblies to have more power. At the
same time, in Paris in the organs of the French Union,
especially the Union, there will have to grow both more
responsibility and status if representation there is to mean
anything to Africans. It will be interesting to see in the
future whether France can develop a political structure
that will bind her colonial peoples with her in an imperial structure and yet offer sufficient political power on
the local level to satisfy her African and other peoples.

Apart from this interesting experiment of the French
Union, there have been important reforms and developments in the economic field. Since 1945 France has spent
three quarters of a billion dollars in West and Equatorial
Africa. This has been done by a means like Britain's
Colonial Development and Welfare Fund, the FIDES
(The Investment Fund for Economic and Social Development) and the Caisse Centrale. The home government's
share is usually 55% of the financing of any develop-
mental project, and to this the colonial government adds
the remaining 45%. In West Africa there are many signs
of economic advance. The territory is producing larger
amounts than ever before of palm kernels, coffee, cocoa,
palm oil, timber, and bananas, and a start has been made
with iron ore and bauxite. Industry of a secondary nature is slowly expanding in such fields as oil-seed crush-
ing, extraction of phosphates, soap making, cement, etc.
The best evidence of this progress can be seen in the
federal capital, Dakar, now a city of 30,000 Europeans
and 250,000 Africans. Its progress has been phenomenal.
Great sums have been spent in improving its harbor, its
airfield, and its public buildings.

No Color Bar in French Africa. French immigration has increased substantially; the European population of French West Africa in 1955 exceeded 60,000. Unlike the situation in British West Africa where the European population is small, composed as it is of the higher colonial officials, missionaries, and key businessmen in a few large trading concerns, in French West Africa there is a large number of petty French businessmen and artisans making their living as tradesmen, bakers, shopkeepers, mechanics, etc. These Europeans are doing much to develop the country. And most important, they mingle with the Africans giving the impression of racial harmony; for unlike British Africa in general and the Union of South Africa in particular, the French territories know little of the color bar. Intermarriage between the African elite and the French is not uncommon. In the long run this racial equality of Black and White, so long as all are French in culture, should go far in eliminating some of the tragic problems and frustrations that are plaguing other parts of Africa.

Like West Africa, Equatorial Africa has witnessed important economic programs of development since 1945. Social and educational services have been expanded and a number of important economic projects carried out. All of these are managed by the governmental agency already mentioned—FIDES. There has been research in new crops, especially rice and cotton, and ports and airfields have been improved. Some improvements have also been made in communications—the greatest need of the territory.

Spain and Portugal in Africa. Only the briefest mention can be made of two other nations that are colonial powers in that part of Africa we have been discussing. These are Spain and Portugal. The first plays an inconsequential role with its west African possession of Spanish Sahara, made up mainly of the colony of Rio de Oro; and in the Gulf of Guinea there is the colony of Spanish Guinea on the mainland, as well as several small islands, principally that of Fernando Poo. We can dismiss these diminutive and undeveloped possessions of Spain with a bare mention, but those of Portugal are more important.

Portugal rules over 300,000 square miles of East

Africa, in Mozambique, and 500,000 square miles of
West Africa, in Angola, populated altogether by some
9,000,000 Africans. The most striking fact about Portuguese Africa is its economic stagnation. There has been
little development, and up to quite recently the only
large-scale enterprises have been the Benguela Railway in
Angola and the Rhodesia and Nyasaland Railway, both
made possible by British capital. One can say that Angola
and Mozambique are the most backward colonies in
Africa. Strategically and economically, however, they are
potentially very important. It will be remembered that
old imperial Germany always had its eyes acquisitively
directed toward Mozambique and Angola. In these colonies are key strategic ports: Lourenço Marques and
Beira, Lobito and Luanda. And today the only west-east
transportation link in Central Africa is the rail lines that
run from Lobito on the Atlantic via the Belgian Congo
and the Rhodesias, ending on the coast of the Indian
Ocean at Lourenço Marques and Beira.

The Portuguese have a colonial policy very much like
the French policy of assimilation. (*See Reading No. 34.*)
There is no idea of ultimate separation of the overseas
possessions from the mother country. Here every African
is potentially a Portuguese citizen. The empire must remain one unit. In order to become a citizen the African
must become a Roman Catholic and must show that he
can read and write Portuguese and has a standard of
living decidedly above that of the tribal African. (*See
Reading No. 35.*) Of all the colonial powers, Portugal
in racial policy has the minimum color bar. Intermarriage
between Black and White is frequent and the only discrimination shown is on the basis of civilization, not
color. Lack of financial resources have seriously impeded
the implementation of this assimilationist policy. There
are not enough schools, not enough economic opportunities, to produce a large African elite that has become
thoroughly European. In Angola, for example, there are
about 140,000 Africans who enjoy full Portuguese citizenship out of a population of 4,000,000. The darkest blot
on the colonial escutcheon of Portugal is recourse to
forced labor for the government, both in Angola and in
Mozambique. Much of this stems from the lack of financial resources and not from "evil intention." The most

urgent need of Portugal is for capital to develop the
resources that are undoubtedly in her African possessions.
If this could be obtained, her colonies might advance
rapidly, and because of the absence of racial discrimination in colonial policy, there would likely be more harmony than has been the case in territories like Kenya
and the Union of South Africa.

— 7 —

CONCLUSION: THE AFRICAN AWAKENING

Continent in Transition. A tour of Africa's main territories from Dakar to Nairobi and from Kampala to
Johannesburg gives ample evidence today of what can be
called *the African awakening.* On every hand there is
the spirit and the manifestation of change—political, social, and economic. Rapid changes bring tensions, fears,
and injustices; and these in turn bring controversy and
the clash of contending ideas. Americans have never been
reluctant to criticize imperialism in general, and are not
now slow to criticize colonialism in Africa in particular.
To our minds self-determination, independence for all
people immediately, is the only way to remove the strife
now convulsing North Africa or to obviate it in the rest
of the continent.

This traditional American viewpoint, however, has
been of late undergoing some modification. As a people
we are beginning to realize that the colonial problem has
been oversimplified, that mere independence does not
necessarily mean the end of problems but in fact may in-
tensify them. For example, "freedom" for the Burmese
and the Indonesians is still on trial, with the future of

the latter people in particular very much in the balance. Independence for India brought the partition of the country and an unnatural sundering of the economic unity of the Indian subcontinent. Whatever moral indictments may be brought against colonial powers for their creation of empires in the past, it serves neither the general tranquillity of the world nor the welfare of the people concerned to give them self-determination before the essential conditions for stable and progressive nationhood have been achieved.

The British Gamble.   The British have gone further than any other African power in passing over the reins of government when it appeared that an influential, albeit small, minority of Westernized Africans was insistent on self-determination. There is no doubt that this is a gigantic gamble. As Professor Margery Perham, the colonial specialist, has observed: "There is no precedent for the sudden grant of the parliamentary franchise to a large, illiterate, tribal population, utterly remote from the political experience of Western Peoples." The African today is too prone to take for granted the law and order, the efficiency and rectitude of the civil service, and above all, the political unity of the country in which he lives. He forgets the primitive conditions and even horrors of a life that was often "nasty, brutish, and short." It is desirable for Africans, and indeed for all those interested in the future of this people's continent, to review occasionally the positive results of colonialism. (*See Readings Nos. 36 and 37.*)

Already there is some disquieting evidence in British West Africa, as we have already noted, of serious problems that may follow in the wake of self-government. It is evident in the Gold Coast, in Nigeria, and to some extent in Sierra Leone that the unity given to these territories came with European rule; and that without it there may follow some form of partition and even fragmentation. And even if political unity can be perpetuated there are doubts, mingled of course with hopes, about the ability and the restraint essential on the part of the educated minority in making self-government a success. There must not only be care to curb corruption and to bridle demagogy in politics, but the leaders who are Westernized must, in most cases, respect the views and

needs of the tribal Africans. "If there is not to be dis-
illusionment with the educated group as leaders, it must
mean an end of condescension toward traditional African
customs, and a sincere and studied attempt to represent
the interests of the majority, and not only the wage
laborers and the elite." [13]

Necessity for Cooperation.   Various kinds of colonial
policy have been examined in this study. But whether
the type of colonial rule be Belgian, French, or British,
it can be said that the African and the European need
to work together. If Africa's problems of poverty, illiteracy, superstition, and ill-health are to be rectified, huge
amounts of capital and managerial skill must be obtained
from Europe and from the United States. African economic backwardness is tied in with tribal customs and
primitive attitudes. In addition, while Africa does have
promising resources, there are certain obstacles to development such as plant and animal diseases, shallowness
of soil, and the like that are almost insoluble if tackled
by the African alone. Related to specifics, this means
that where self-government has been obtained, leaders
such as Nkrumah in the Gold Coast would do well to
continue some form of consultation and partnership with
Britain. In the case of plural societies such as Kenya
and the Federation of Rhodesia and Nyasaland, the
problem is much more difficult. In such territories it is
the European settler community that must have vision.
There are signs in Kenya and the Rhodesias that a new
attitude is forming among the settlers. Recently, a leading
European member of the Rhodesian Federal Parliament
warned his fellow-Europeans that they must see clearly
what sacrifices they should be prepared to make if their
multiracial state was to succeed. He concluded: "There
are in theory two possible courses to follow—to work
together with all that implies and to work apart with all
that implies. In theory, either must succeed, but it must
be either one or the other, and not a combination of
both." [14]

The Problem of Apartheid.   There remains the
multiracial state of the Union of South Africa. As in

---

[13] Ralph Linton, ed., *Most of the World* (Columbia University
Press, New York, 1949) p. 398.

[14] *The New York Times,* August 28, 1955, p. 36.

Kenya and the Rhodesias, only more so, the shape of
things to come rests primarily in the hands and hearts
of the European population. Undoubtedly this territory
is potentially the most explosive in all Africa south of the
Sahara. The bulk of liberal opinion outside of the Union
is inclined to believe that the policy of *apartheid,* as at
present interpreted, is not only unjust to the African but
in the long run will not give the European minority the
security it so desperately seeks. It can only lead to
tragedy, to an internal convulsion. But this verdict does
not give the outsider the right to criticize without sym-
pathy, to point the finger without humility. In the case
of Americans, with a problem of color or race insignifi-
cant as compared to South Africa's, we should ask ourselves what still remains to be done to solve our own
problem.

Africa and the Future.   Africa on occasion has been
called Tomorrow's Continent. Today the pressure and
complexity of its problems would seem to rule out this
prospect for a long period of time. Any undue pessimism
might be corrected by having the right time perspective.
In little more than fifty years, Africans in many parts of
the continent have bridged the gap between cannibalism
and industrialism. In the Congo, barely exposed to civilization half a century ago, many natives are now working
in mines producing uranium for an atomic age. The
author has met cultivated African medical doctors whose
parents lived in isolated, primitive villages in the native
reserves of South Africa. If these amazing changes have
taken place in such a short time, another fifty years may
see a substantial rectification of those obstacles and
problems that now disturb the tranquillity of Africa and
stand in the way of its admission into the family of the
world's great continents.

Part II

READINGS

— Reading No. 1 —

STANLEY FINDS LIVINGSTONE, 1872[1]

Since the time that Dr. Livingstone went into Central Africa in 1866, no direct word had been received from him and there was much conjecture as to his fate. In 1870 the famous journalist H. M. Stanley was commissioned by the New York Herald to "find" the famous missionary-explorer. Plunging into the jungle early in 1871, Stanley and his party searched for 236 days before Livingstone was located at Ujiji on the shores of Lake Tanganyika.

We push on rapidly, lest the news of our coming might reach the people of Bunder Ujiji before we come in sight, and are ready for them. . . . The port of Ujiji is below us, embowered in the palms, only five hundred yards from us. At this grand moment we do not think of the hundreds of miles we have marched, of the hundreds of hills we have ascended and descended, of the many forests we have traversed, of the jungles and thickets that annoyed us, of the fervid salt plains that blistered our feet, of the hot suns that scorched us, nor of the dangers and difficulties, now happily surmounted. At last the sublime hour has arrived!—our dreams, our hopes, and anticipations are now about to be realized! Our hearts and our feelings are with our eyes, as we peer into the palms and try to make out in which hut or house lives the white man with the grey beard we heard about on the Malagarazi. . . .

Unfurl the flags, and load your guns!

Ay Wallah, ay Wallah, bana! respond the men eagerly.

[1] Condensed from Henry Morton Stanley, *How I Found Livingstone in Central Africa* (New York, 1872) pp. 402-425.

One, two, three,—fire! . . . .

Now hold the white man's flag up high, and let the
Zanzibar flag bring up the rear. And you men keep close
together, and keep firing until we halt in the market
place, or before the white man's house. You have said to
me often that you could smell the fish of the Tanganyika
—I can smell the fish of the Tanganyika now. There
are fish and beer, and a long rest waiting for you.
MARCH! . . .

But by this time we were within two hundred yards of
the village, and the multitude was getting denser, and
almost preventing our march. Flags and streamers were
out . . . and Selim [Stanley's servant] said to me, "I see
the Doctor, sir. Oh, what an old man! He has got a
white beard." . . . My heart beats fast, but I must not
let my face betray my emotions, lest it shall detract from
the dignity of a white man appearing under such extra-
ordinary circumstances.

So I did what I thought was most dignified. I pushed
back the crowds, and, passing from the rear, walked
down a living avenue of people, until I came in front of
the semicircle of Arabs, in the front of which stood the
white man with the grey beard. As I advanced slowly towards him I noticed he was pale, looked worried, had a
grey beard, wore a bluish cap with a faded gold band
around it, had on a red-sleeved waistcoat, and a pair of
grey tweed trousers. I would have run to him, only I was
a coward in the presence of such a mob—would have
embraced him, only, he being an Englishman, I did not
know how he would receive me; so I did what cowardice
and false pride suggested was the best thing—walked
deliberately to him, took off my hat, and said: "Dr.
Livingstone, I presume?"

"Yes," said he, with a kind smile, lifting his cap
slightly.

I replace my hat on my head, and he puts on his cap,
and we both grasp hands, and then I say aloud:

"I thank God, Doctor, that I have been permitted to
see you."

He answered, "I feel thankful that I am here to welcome you.". . .

The Doctor kept the letter-bag on his knee, then,
presently, opened it, looked at the letters contained there,

and read one or two of his children's letters, his face in the meanwhile lighting up.

He asked me to tell him the news. "No, Doctor," said I, "read your letters first, which I am sure you must be impatient to read."

"Ah," said he, "I have waited years for letters, and I have been taught patience. I can surely afford to wait a few hours longer. No, tell me the general news: how is the world getting along?"

"You probably know much already. Do you know that the Suez Canal is a fact—is opened, and a regular trade carried on between Europe and India through it?"

"I did not hear about the opening of it. Well, that is grand news! What else?"

Shortly I found myself enacting the part of an annual periodical to him. There was no need of exaggeration. . . . The world had witnessed and experienced much the last few years. The Pacific Railroad had been completed; Grant had been elected President of the United States; Egypt had been flooded with savants; the Cretan rebellion had terminated; a Spanish revolution had driven Isabella from the throne of Spain . . . Prussia had humbled Denmark, and annexed Schleswig-Holstein, and her armies were around Paris; the "Man of Destiny" was a prisoner . . . the Queen of fashion and the Empress of the French was a fugitive . . . the Napoleon dynasty was extinguished by the Prussians, Bismarck and Von Moltke; and France, the proud empire, was humbled to the dust. . . .

"Doctor," I said, "you had better read your letters. I will not keep you up any longer." . . . This was the beginning of our life at Ujiji. I knew him not as a friend before my arrival. He was only an object to me—a great item for a daily newspaper. . . . I had gone over battle-fields, witnessed revolutions, civil wars, rebellions, émeutes and massacres; stood close to the condemned murderer to record his last struggles and last sighs; but never had I been called to record anything that moved me so much as this man's woes and sufferings, his privations and disappointments, which now were poured into my ear.

— Reading No. 2 —

TREATY MAKING IN AFRICA [2]

An American student of imperialism shows how a noted English explorer, Sir Harry Johnston, obtained land from the native African chiefs during the hectic scramble for territory by the European powers.

In a long native canoe Johnston and his forty Kruboys [Negro porters] and Callabars paddled up the Cross River, through lonely glades, startling an occasional chimpanzee or elephant herd, but seeing no human beings, until they neared a large Negro village. Savages rushed out into the water, dragged Johnston from his canoe, and carried him off to a native hut. There, with a hundred human skulls grinning at him from the walls, he had to sit, while a crowd of savages stared at his strange complexion and clothes. At length his captors questioned him, through his native interpreter. He came, he said, on a friendly mission from "a great white Queen who was the ruler of the White People." He wished to "make a book" with the ruler of the village—that is, a treaty—to "take home to the Woman Chief" who had sent him out. The natives, fortunately, were agreeable. A burly individual carried him back to the canoe, and there Johnston took a treaty form [he had a stock ready for such contingencies] from his dispatch box, while three or four Negroes, apparently persons of authority, crowded into the canoe to make crosses on the treaty. The natives, it seemed, had consumed enough palm-wine to be genial, even boisterous. Seeing their condition, Johnston "was longing to get away." Accordingly, "after the crosses had been splodged on the treaty-form" and he had given them a present of beads and cloth, he made his adieus, but not before the villagers had generously compelled him to accept a hundred yams and two sheep—and "a necklace of human knuckle bones." Then, fearing that the natives might kill and eat his servants, Johnston made "a judicious retreat."

[2] Parker Thomas Moon, *Imperialism and World Politics* (The Macmillan Co., New York, 1944) p. 101. Reprinted by permission of The Macmillan Company.

THE BERLIN ACT, 1885[3]

On the invitation of Prince Bismarck for the Imperial German Government, the interested powers met in Berlin in 1884 and early the next spring produced the Berlin Act. Its purpose was to lay down principles for the freedom of trade and navigation in the Congo region, for the suppression of the slave trade, for the furtherance of the well-being of the natives, and for principles regulating fresh acts of occupation by the great powers.

ꞌ   ꞌ   ꞌ

Freedom of Trade to All Nations

ARTICLE I. The trade of all nations shall enjoy complete freedom. . . .

No Taxes to be Levied on Wares Imported (*with Slight Exceptions*)

ARTICLE III. Wares, of whatever origin, imported into these regions, under whatsoever flag, by sea or river, or overland, shall be subject to no other taxes than such as may be levied as fair compensation for expenditure in the interests of trade, and which for this reason must be equally borne by the subjects themselves and by foreigners of all nationalities.

No Import or Transit Duties to Be Levied

ARTICLE IV. Merchandise imported into these regions shall remain free from import and transit dues. . . .

ARTICLE VI. *Provisions Relative to Protection of the Natives, of Missionaries and Travellers, as well as Relative to Religious Liberty*

[3] Extracts from the General Appendices. Cited in Raymond Leslie Buell, *The Native Problem in Africa* (The Macmillan Co., New York, 1928) II, pp. 891-907. Reprinted by permission of The Macmillan Company.

Preservation and Improvement of Native Tribes; Slavery, and the Slave Trade

All the powers exercising sovereign rights or influence in the aforesaid territories bind themselves to watch over the preservation of the native tribes, and to care for the improvement of the conditions of their moral and material well-being, and to help in suppressing slavery, and especially the slave trade.

Religious and Other Institutions. Civilization of Natives

They shall, without distinction of creed or nation, protect and favour all religious, scientific, or charitable institutions, and undertakings created and organized for the above ends, or which aim at instructing the natives and bringing home to them the blessings of civilization.

Protection of Missionaries, Scientists, and Explorers

Christian missionaries, scientists, and explorers, with their followers, property, and collections, shall likewise be the objects of especial protection.

Religious Toleration

Freedom of conscience and religious toleration are expressly guaranteed to the natives, no less than to subjects and to foreigners.

Public Worship

The free and public exercise of all forms of Divine worship, and the right to build edifices for religious purposes, and to organize religious missions belonging to all creeds, shall not be limited or fettered in any way whatsoever. . . .

Suppression of the Slave Trade by Land and Sea; and of Slave Markets

ARTICLE IX. Seeing that trading in slaves is forbidden in conformity with the principles of international law as recognized by the Signatory Powers, and seeing also that the operations, which, by sea or land, furnish slaves to trade, ought likewise to be regarded as forbidden, the Powers which do or shall exercise sovereign rights or influence in the territories forming the Conventional basin

of the Congo declare that these territories may not serve
as a market or means of transit for the trade in slaves, of
whatever race they may be. Each of the Powers binds
itself to employ all means at its disposal for putting an
end to this trade and for punishing those who engage in
it. . . .

Notification of Acquisitions and Protectorates on Coasts of African Continent

ARTICLE XXXIV. Any power which henceforth takes
possession of a tract of land on the coasts of the African
continent outside of its present possessions, or which,
hitherto without such possessions, shall acquire them, as
well as the Power which assumes a Protectorate there,
shall accompany the respective act with a notification
thereof, addressed to the other Signatory Powers of the
present Act, in order to enable them, if need be, to make
good any claims of their own.

Establishment of Authority in Territories Occupied on Coasts, Protection of Existing Rights. Freedom of Trade and Transit

ARTICLE XXXV. The Signatory Powers of the present
Act recognize the obligation to insure the establishment
of authority in regions occupied by them on the coasts
of the African continent sufficient to protect existing
rights, and, as the case may be, freedom of trade and of
transit under the conditions agreed upon.

— Reading No. 4 —

THE CONGO ATROCITIES[4]

[4] Extracts from Ludwig Bauer, *Leopold The Unloved* (Little,
Brown & Company, Boston, 1935), pp. 263, 264, and 269-
270.

*A biographer of Leopold II, King of the Belgians, cites
testimony of eyewitnesses to the horrible cruelties prac-
tised in the Congo Free State by the avaricious rubber
traders.*

✔   ✔   ✔

Lieutenant Tilkens writes [in letters]: "Commandant
Verstraeten visited my station and congratulated me
warmly. He said his report would depend upon the quantity of rubber which I was able to provide. The quantity
increased from 360 kilogrammes in September to 1500 in
October, and from January onwards it will amount to
4000 per month, which will bring me in a monthly pre-
mium of 500 francs. Am I not a lucky fellow? If I go on
like this, within two years I shall have earned premiums
of 12,000 Fcs." He continues: "S.S. *Van Kerkhoven* is
coming down the Nile and will demand 1500 Porters.
Unlucky niggers! I can hardly bear to think of them. I
am asking myself how on earth I shall be able to hunt up
so large a number." Then: "Marshes, hunger, exhaustion. How much blood will be shed because of this transport! Three times, already, I have had to make war
upon the chiefs who would not help me to get the men
I needed. The fellows would rather die in their own
forests than as members of a transport train. If a chief
refuses, that means war, with modern fire-arms on one
side against spears and javelins on the other!" . . .

Senator Picard . . . travelled in the Congo Free State.
Here are his impressions: "The inhabitants have disappeared. Their homes have been burned; huge heaps of
ashes amid neglected palm-hedges and devastated aban-
doned fields. Inhuman floggings, murders, plunderings,
and carryings-off. . . ." And: "The people flee into the
wild or seek protection in French or Portuguese territory." Near Stanley Pool on the caravan road he notices:
"A continual succession of blacks, carrying loads upon
their heads; worn-out beasts of burden, with projecting
joints, wasted features, and staring eyes, perpetually trying to keep afoot despite their exhaustion. By thousands
they pass, in the service of the State, handed over by
the chiefs, whose slaves they are and who rob them of
their wages. They totter along the road, with bent knees
and protruding bellies, crawling with vermin, a dreadful

procession across hill and dale, dying from exhaustion by the wayside, or often succumbing even should they reach home after their wanderings." . . .

Here are extracts from the reports of a commission which travelled through the whole State, compiled from the declarations of eye-witnesses. . . . "Within the territories of the Abir, the chief Isekifasu of Bolima was murdered, his wife and children being eaten by the cannibal guards; the houses of the natives were decorated with the intestines, the liver, and the heart of the murdered. . . . The successor of the murdered chief . . . attended by twenty witnesses, comes and lays a hundred and ten twigs upon the table, each of them signifying a murder for rubber. . . . The soldiers had shown him the corpses of his people saying: 'Now you will bring us rubber!' " So it goes on: "Children have their brains dashed out; murders without ceasing; the bodies of the slain are eaten; soldiers are flogged by the agents' orders if they have been slack in the work of murder; women mutilated because they are true to their husbands. The commission spends many hours, many days, listening to such reports. . . . Behind each who complains, stand hundreds who do not dare to speak, or lie hundreds of slain who will never speak again. The wailings from the Congo are slow and repressed, but, irresistibly, the cry grows."

— Reading No. 5 —

MANDATES AND THE LEAGUE OF NATIONS, 1919 [5]

Article 22 of the Covenant of the League of Nations laid down the general philosophy underlying the mandate

[5] Cited in Raymond Leslie Buell, *The Native Problem in Africa* (The Macmillan Co., New York, 1928) I, 545–546. Reprinted by permission of The Macmillan Company.

system. The various categories of mandates were defined, the administering mandatory powers agreed to present an annual report of their activities, and the general mandate system was to be supervised by a permanent mandates commission.

✓   ✓   ✓

1. To those colonies and territories which as a consequence of the late war have ceased to be under the sovereignty of the States which formerly governed them and which are inhabited by peoples not yet able to stand by themselves under the strenuous conditions of the modern world, there should be applied the principle that the well-being and development of such peoples form a sacred trust of civilization and that securities for the performance of this trust should be embodied in this Covenant.

2. The best method of giving practical effect to this principle is that the tutelage of such peoples should be intrusted to advanced nations who, by reason of their resources, their experience or their geographical position, can best undertake this responsibility, and who are willing to accept it, and that this tutelage should be exercised by them as Mandatories on behalf of the League.

3. The character of the mandate must differ according to the stage of the development of the people, the geographical situation of the territory, its economic conditions and other similar circumstances.

4. Certain communities formerly belonging to the Turkish Empire have reached a stage of development where their existence as independent nations can be provisionally recognized subject to the rendering of administrative advice and assistance by a Mandatory until such time as they are able to stand alone. The wishes of these communities must be a principal consideration in the selection of the Mandatory.

5. Other peoples, especially those of Central Africa, are at such a stage that the Mandatory must be responsible for the administration of the territory under conditions which will guarantee freedom of conscience and religion, subject only to the maintenance of public order and morals, the prohibition of abuses such as the slave trade, the arms traffic and the liquor traffic, and the prevention

of the establishment of fortifications or military and naval bases and of military training of natives for other than police purposes and the defense of the territory, and will also secure equal opportunities for the trade and commerce of other Members of the League.

6. There are territories, such as Southwest Africa and certain of the South Pacific islands, which, owing to the sparseness of their population or their small size, or their remoteness from the centers of civilization, or their geographical contiguity to the territory of the Mandatory, and other circumstances, can be best administered under the laws of the Mandatory as integral portions of its territory, subject to the safeguards above mentioned in the interests of the indigenous population.

7. In every case of mandate, the Mandatory shall render to the Council an annual report in reference to the territory committed to its charge.

8. The degree of authority, control or administration to be exercised by the Mandatory shall, if not previously agreed upon by the Members of the League, be explicitly defined in each case by the Council.

9. A permanent Commission shall be constituted to receive and examine the annual reports of the Mandatories, and to advise the Council on all matters relating to the observance of the mandates.

— Reading No. 6 —

THE BRITISH MANDATE FOR GERMAN EAST AFRICA, 1922[6]

Allotted by the Big Four to Great Britain at the Paris Peace Conference in 1919, German East Africa, now to

[6] *League of Nations, Official Journal*, Third Year (Geneva, 1922) pp. 865-868.

be known as Tanganyika, was the most important man-
date taken from Germany and given to one of the victors.
In addition, a small area of the former German protect-
orate Ruanda-Urundi was turned over to Belgium to
administer. The following document is the text of the
British mandate specifying the obligations and conditions
under which the mandatory was to operate.

ARTICLE 3. The Mandatory shall be responsible for the
peace, order and good government of the territory, and
shall undertake to promote to the utmost the material and
moral well-being and the social progress of its inhabitants.
The Mandatory shall have full powers of legislation and
administration.

ARTICLE 4. The Mandatory shall not establish any military or naval bases, nor erect any fortifications, nor organise any native military force in the territory except
for local police purposes and for the defence of the
territory.

ARTICLE 5. The Mandatory:

(1) shall provide for the eventual emancipation of all
    slaves and for as speedy an elimination of domes-
    tic and other slavery as social conditions will
    allow;
(2) shall suppress all forms of slave trade;
(3) shall prohibit all forms of forced or compulsory
    labour, except for essential public works and serv-
    ices, and then only in return for adequate re-
    muneration;
(4) shall protect the natives from abuse and measures
    of fraud and force by the careful supervision of
    labour contracts and the recruiting of labour;
(5) shall exercise a strict control over the traffic in
    arms and ammunition and the sale of spirituous
    liquors.

ARTICLE 6. In the framing of laws relating to the holding or transfer of land, the Mandatory shall take into
consideration native laws and customs, and shall respect
the rights and safeguard the interests of the native population.

No native land may be transferred, except between
natives, without the previous consent of the public au-

thorities, and no real rights over native land in favour of non-natives may be created except with the same consent.

The Mandatory will promulgate strict regulations against usury.

ARTICLE 7. The Mandatory shall secure to all nationals of States Members of the League of Nations the same rights as are enjoyed in the territory by his own nationals. . . .

The rights conferred by this article extend equally to companies and associations organised in accordance with the law of any of the Members of the League of Nations. . . .

ARTICLE 8. The Mandatory shall ensure in the territory complete freedom of conscience and the free exercise of all forms of worship which are consonant with public order and morality. . . .

ARTICLE 9. The Mandatory shall apply to the territory any general international conventions already existing . . . respecting the slave-trade, the traffic in arms and ammunition, the liquor traffic, and the traffic in drugs, or relating to commercial equality, freedom of transit and navigation, aerial navigation, railways, postal, telegraphic, and wireless communication, and industrial, literary and artistic property.

The Mandatory shall co-operate in the execution of any common policy adopted by the League of Nations for preventing and combating disease, including diseases of plants and animals.

ARTICLE 10. The Mandatory shall be authorised to constitute the territory into a customs fiscal and administrative union or federation with the adjacent territories under his own sovereignty or control; provided always that the measures adopted to that end do not infringe the provisions of this mandate.

ARTICLE 11. The Mandatory shall make to the Council of the League of Nations an annual report to the satisfaction of the Council, containing full information concerning the measures taken to apply the provisions of this mandate. . . .

ARTICLE 12. The consent of the Council of the League of Nations is required for any modification of the terms of this mandate.

ARTICLE 13. The Mandatory agrees that if any dispute

should arise between the Mandatory and another Member of the League of Nations . . . such dispute, if it cannot be settled by negotiation, shall be submitted to the Permanent Court of International Justice.

— Reading No. 7 —

OBJECTIVES OF THE INTERNATIONAL INSTITUTE OF AFRICAN LANGUAGES AND CULTURES, 1926[7]

As a result of the new interest in Africa following World War I, a number of scholars and colonial officials established an institute designed to study the many complex problems of this continent. The project was a truly international one, for experts from the principal colonial powers—and from Germany—cooperated to set it in motion. It was rightly claimed "that a new era of international cooperation in the service of Africa was now opened." The major purposes of the Institute were defined in its constitution.

✶   ✶   ✶

To study the languages and cultures of the natives of Africa.

To give advice and aid in the publication of studies on African languages, folk-lore, and art.

To constitute a bureau of information for bodies and persons interested in linguistic and ethnological researches and educational work in Africa.

[7] "The Story of the Institute," *Africa* (London), January 1934, p. 4.

To make and carry out any arrangement for joint working or cooperation with any other society or body having objects similar to those of the Institute.

To assist in the production of an educational literature in the vernacular. . . .

To promote an understanding of African languages and social institutions. . . .

To encourage international cooperation in all questions connected with the mental development and technical advancement of the people of Africa.

— Reading No. 8 —

BRITISH NATIVE POLICY IN EAST AFRICA, 1923[8]

Following World War I, the British settlers in Kenya were aroused over proposals to give Indians the vote in a general electorate, restricted by a common educational and property test. The settlers threatened open revolt. In reply the British Government issued a white paper withdrawing the Indian proposals but also enunciating the doctrine that the interests of the native population must be paramount. This is a famous statement of colonial policy.

Primarily, Kenya is an African territory, and His Majesty's Government think it necessary definitely to record their considered opinion that the interests of the African natives must be paramount, and that if, and when, those interests and the interests of the immigrant races should conflict, the former should prevail. Ob-

[8] *Indians in Kenya,* Cmd. 1922 (London, 1923). Reprinted by permission of the Controller, Her Britannic Majesty's Stationery Office.

viously the interests of the other communities, European, Indian, or Arab, must severally be safeguarded. Whatever the circumstances in which members of these communities have entered Kenya, there will be no drastic action or reversal of measures already introduced . . . the result of which might be to destroy or impair the existing interests of those who have already settled in Kenya. But in the administration of Kenya His Majesty's Government regard themselves as exercising a trust on behalf of the African population, and they are unable to delegate or share this trust, the object of which may be defined as the protection and advancement of the native races. It is not necessary to attempt to elaborate this position; the lines of development are as yet in certain directions undetermined, and many difficult problems arise which require time for their solution. But there can be no room for doubt that it is the mission of Great Britain to work continuously for the training and education of the Africans towards a higher intellectual, moral and economic level than that which they had reached when the Crown assumed the responsibility for the administration of this territory. At present special consideration is being given to economic development in the native reserves, and within the limits imposed by the finances of the Colony all that is possible for the advancement and development of the Africans, both inside and outside the native reserves, will be done. . . .

It has been suggested that it might be possible for Kenya to advance in the near future on the lines of responsible self-government, subject to the reservation of native affairs. There are, however, in the opinion of His Majesty's Government, objections to the adoption in Kenya at this stage of such an arrangement . . . and they are convinced that the existing system of government is, in present circumstances, best calculated to achieve the aims which they have in view, namely, the unfettered exercise of their trusteeship for the native races and the satisfaction of the legitimate aspirations of other communities resident in the Colony.

— Reading No. 9 —

BRITAIN'S DUAL MANDATE IN AFRICA JUSTIFIED, 1926[9]

Lord Lugard, creator of indirect rule *in colonial administration, author and authority on native policy, defines the* dual mandate, *the concept that Britain is in Africa both for her own enlightened self-interest and for the advancement of the African people.*

✓   ✓   ✓

Let it be admitted at the outset that European brains, capital, and energy have not been, and never will be, expended in developing the resources of Africa from motives of pure philanthropy; that Europe is in Africa for the mutual benefit of her own industrial classes, and of the native races in their progress to a higher plane; that the benefit can be made reciprocal, and that it is the aim and desire of civilized administration to fulfill this dual mandate.

By railroads and roads, by reclamation of swamps and irrigation of deserts, and by a system of fair trade and competition, we have added to the prosperity and wealth of these lands, and checked famine and disease. We have put an end to the awful misery of the slave-trade and inter-tribal war, to human sacrifice and the ordeals of the witch-doctor. . . . We are endeavouring to teach the native races to conduct their own affairs with justice and humanity, and to educate them alike in letters and in industry.

When I recall the state of Uganda at the time I made the treaty in 1890 which brought it under British control, or the state of Nigeria ten years later, and contrast them with the conditions of to-day, I feel that British effort—

[9] F. D. Lugard, *The Dual Mandate in British Tropical Africa* (William Blackwood & Sons, Ltd., Edinburgh, 1926) pp. 617-618. Reprinted by permission of William Blackwood & Sons, Ltd.

apart from benefits to British trade—has not been in vain. In Uganda a triangular civil war was raging—Protestants, Roman Catholics, and Moslems, representing the rival political factions of British, French, and Arabs, were murdering each other. Only a short time previously triumphant paganism had burnt Christians at the stake and revelled in holocausts of victims. To-day there is an ordered Government with its own native parliament. Liberty and Justice have replaced chaos, bloodshed, and war. The wealth of the country steadily increases. The slave-raids and tyranny of the neighbouring kingdom of Unyoro have given place to similar progress and peace.

In Nigeria in 1902 slave-raiding armies of 10,000 or 15,000 men laid waste the country, and wiped out its population annually in the quest of slaves. Hundreds of square miles of rich well-watered land were depopulated. . . . Nowhere was there security for life and property. To-day the native Emirs vie with each other in the progress of their schools; the native courts administer justice, and themselves have liberated over 50,000 slaves. . . .

I refer to these two countries because I happen to have personally witnessed their condition prior to the advent of British control, but similar results may be seen in every other British dependency in tropical Africa.

As Roman imperialism laid the foundations of modern civilisation, and led the wild barbarians of these islands along the path of progress, so in Africa to-day we are re-paying the debt, and bringing to the dark places of the earth, the abode of barbarism and cruelty, the torch of culture and progress, while administering to the material needs of our own civilisation.

— Reading No. 10 —

GENERAL CONSIDERATIONS AFFECTING WHITE SETTLEMENT, 1931 [10]

[10] Joint Committee on Closer Union in East Africa, *Report* (London, 1931) I, 23-25. Reprinted by permission of the Controller, Her Britannic Majesty's Stationery Office.

In 1931 a joint committee of both houses of the British Parliament exhaustively studied and issued a report on the problems of East Africa. One of the sections of this document analyzed the pros and cons of white settlement, with particular reference to Kenya.

✓   ✓   ✓

The presence of a settled white community in East Africa raises problems fundamental to the Committee's whole inquiry. The question how far, and subject to what conditions, we, as a nation, are justified in encouraging the settlement of our own people in a country already inhabited by a native population is one which must be fairly faced. To deny that justification in general terms would lead to the conclusion that the North American and Australian continents should have been strictly for the aboriginal populations. To affirm it without qualification would involve the denial of any rights or fair opportunities for development of whole categories of human beings on the ground of their present weakness or relative inefficiency, and would mean the repudiation of the whole doctrine of trusteeship upon which the Empire is professedly based. The principle of trusteeship implies not only the avoidance of direct injustice to the natives as individuals but also the more positive obligation to afford to the natives, as a race, both time and opportunity to develop their latent capacities and play such a part as they may eventually prove capable of playing in the ultimate destiny of the country. Every opportunity for advancement should moreover be afforded to such natives as may reach a higher level than is common to their race.

In the case of East Africa there can be no doubt . . . that the introduction of European rule, as distinct from European settlement, has been of great benefit to the native people. The influx of European settlement at the beginning of the century was encouraged by Government in order to promote the development of areas which, partly owing to their relatively colder climate and partly owing to Masai [a warrior tribe] devastation, were largely unoccupied or in very sparse or irregular occupation. The subsequent expansion of European settlement may have led to some transactions of doubtful fairness, and has necessitated effective measures to protect against all future alienations sufficient land to provide for present and prospective native requirements. At the same time it would be difficult to find any other instance of a white population settling in a native country with so little disturbance of the original population. Nor, after making all allowance for a tendency on the part of the settler community to influence the construction of railways or the framing of tariffs and of taxation generally in a direction primarily favourable to the development of areas and industries in which they have been interested, can it be denied that the natives as a whole have benefited from the presence of the settler community.

European settlement in the tropics of East Africa is, of course, an experiment little more than a quarter of a century old, and its success cannot yet be considered as definitely established. In the course of the evidence an interesting analysis of the economic basis on which white settlement has hitherto rested was submitted to the Committee, the general conclusion of which was that white settlement has not really been self-supporting. . . . This view and its implications were opposed by a considerable body of evidence. When allowance is made for the severe set-back which the young settler community suffered owing to the war, and for the difficult economic conditions of the post-war period, the progress made so far certainly compares not unfavourably with that of other countries at the same stage in their history. On the other hand, even when the initial stage of taking root has been overcome, the possibilities of any large expansion would seem to be precluded by the limited area of the temperate highlands as well as by the narrowly restricted sphere of occupations which the white man is prepared to take up. . . .

It is considerations of this kind which emphasize the importance of securing that the development of both races shall be complementary to each other, and the responsibility of His Majesty's Government both in holding the scales even and in endeavouring to foster a similar sense of responsibility in the settler community by enlisting their interest and co-operation in the problems of native administration. Subject to these considerations . . . the Committee wish to affirm their belief in the value of white settlement as an important element in the progress of East Africa, and their hopes for its future success.

— Reading No. 11 —

GERMANY DEMANDS HER COLONIES BACK, 1933[11]

During the 1920's there were rumbles of discontent from Germany over the loss of her colonial empire in 1919. In the 1930's after the rise of Hitler these rumbles became a mighty roar. Here the recent Chancellor of the German Republic eloquently presents his country's case for the return of her colonies.

✓   ✓   ✓

When the German Empire crumbled under the onslaught of twenty-three nations, Germany's colonial empire was sunk without trace. At Versailles, Germany lost her place in the tropical sun. The Allies stripped her of all colonies. . . .

The dictate of Versailles deprived Germany, already cramped, of one-tenth of her continental area and population. Germany must remain crippled unless she gains somewhere that breathing space which she needs to live.

An early revision of the colonial peace terms is not merely a question of prestige; it is a dire necessity. I succeeded at Lausanne in persuading the Allies to wipe reparations off the ledger. Nevertheless, Germany can continue the services and amortization of her so-called short-term loans only if her natural birthright to share in international trade is no longer withheld.

If the Reich is expected to survive, Germany must demand a share in the development of the colonial areas. Germany's title to her place in the tropical sun cannot be doubted in the light of pre-armistice conditions. It is firmly intrenched in the peace treaty itself. . . .

The developments of the past few years demonstrate that Germany cannot put her house economic in order

---

[11] Franz von Papen, "Germany's Place in the Tropical Sun," *The Saturday Evening Post*, September 30, 1933, pp. 23-34.

unless she enjoys unhampered access to tropical raw material and colonial markets. In 1926 Dr. Hjalmar Schacht insisted: "The Dawes Plan cannot be executed unless Germany is allowed a great colonial development." Before the war, the world owed Germany $5,000,000,000. Today the Reich is indebted for the same amount to foreign creditors. Allied statesmen attempt to sidestep the colonial question. . . . But it will not remain on the shelf. . . .

Among the monuments unveiled on the occasion marking half a century of [German] colonization, I was particularly impressed with a gigantic brick elephant erected in Bremen. This behemoth of the jungle symbolizes the enormous natural resources still slumbering in the heart of Africa. It reminds the German people that, among the points in need of revision in the Peace Treaty of Versailles, the question of the German colonies can no longer be slighted. It was my privilege, as chancellor of the Reich, to extend official congratulations to the German Colonial Society on the occasion of its anniversary. . . . It must not be forgotten that Africa . . . includes among its inhabitants a number of tribes and races which are not yet ripe to govern or to manage themselves. Europe is, so to speak, the intellectual guardian of those peoples. To Europe has fallen the great task of bringing to them the blessings of civilization. Should Germany alone be excluded from this mission? I say, "No!" Our right to take part in this work is just as great as that of other civilized nations. . . .

We cannot surrender the few rights left to us in the most humiliating peace treaty ever forced upon a great nation since the destruction of Carthage.

Colonies, I repeat, are an economic necessity for Germany for four reasons:

To feed her own people.

To take care of her surplus population.

To meet her foreign credit engagements, especially her private loans.

To afford her an opportunity of spreading culture and civilization.

The great majority of 65,000,000 Germans refuse to regard their former colonies as lost possessions. They look upon them as territory placed temporarily under the administration of other powers, pending a final settlement. . . .

World stability cannot be established until Germany regains her place in the tropical sun.

— Reading No. 12 —

CHURCHILL, THE COLONIAL EMPIRE, AND THE ATLANTIC CHARTER, 1941 [12]

In the Atlantic Charter President Roosevelt and Prime Minister Churchill had declared that they "respect the right of all peoples to choose the form of government under which they will live, and they wish to see sovereign rights and self-government restored to those who have been deprived of them." This statement was taken by many people in the colonial world as a promise of immediate self-determination. Later, in the House of Commons, the Prime Minister made a statement that aroused opposition in the African colonies and in India. It was interpreted as an exclusion of the colonial peoples from the ideals of the Charter.

ᕃ   ᕃ   ᕃ

The Joint Declaration does not qualify in any way the various statements of policy which have been made from time to time about the development of constitutional government in India, Burma, or other parts of the British Empire. We are pledged by the Declaration of August 1941 to help India to attain free and equal partnership in the British Commonwealth. . . . At the Atlantic meet-

[12] *Great Britain, Parliamentary Debates, House of Commons* (London, 1941).

ing we had in mind, primarily, the restoration of the
sovereignty, [and] self-government . . . of the States
and Nations of Europe now under the Nazi yoke. . . .
So that is quite a separate problem from the progressive
evolution of self-governing institutions in the regions and
peoples which owe allegiance to the British Crown. We
have made declarations on these matters which are complete in themselves, free from ambiguity, and related to
the conditions and circumstances of the territories and
peoples affected. They will be found to be entirely in
harmony with the high conception of freedom and justice
which inspired the Joint Declaration.

— Reading No. 13 —

AFRICA, THE WAR, AND PEACE AIMS, 1942[13]

*The implications of the Atlantic Charter for the future
of colonies were numerous and profound. A number of
organizations endeavored to spell out a program of economic, social, and political advancement for colonial
peoples, reflecting the basic philosophy of the Atlantic
Charter. One of the most penetrating and comprehensive
statements was prepared by the Committee on Africa, the
War, and Peace Aims initiated and sponsored by The
Phelps-Stokes Fund of New York City, an American
foundation long interested in African problems and progress. The Committee's "Summary of Major Findings and
Recommendations" follows.*

✓   ✓   ✓

[13] *The Atlantic Charter and Africa from an American Stand-
point* (New York, 1942) pp. 102-108. Reprinted by permission of The Phelps-Stokes Fund.

Among the Committee's major findings are the following:

That Africa today should be the subject of intelligent study in this country for many reasons, but especially because it is the ancestral home of one tenth of our population, and that it is a continent of vast possibilities and difficult problems, and of vital concern to the United Nations in the present war.

That Africa still represents the largest undeveloped area in the world, with mineral deposits, agricultural land, waterpower, forest and wildlife resources of importance, all of which are decreasing in value because of careless or reckless use or exploitation; and that these resources need development for its own defense and welfare. . . .

That the impact of Western civilization on the primitive culture of Africa has created extremely difficult problems, with resulting credits and debits.

That the native people, although differing widely in their stages of culture, interests, and talents, have large potentiality, and that there is in every colony a steadily increasing group of educated Africans competent to take positions of additional responsibility.

That the missionary societies, both Protestant and Catholic, have in many instances led the way in education, medicine, and other fields, and such organizations as the Institute of Race Relations in the Union of South Africa, have done much for the protection of Africans' rights and interests.

That America has a large interest in Africa—missionary, financial, educational, scientific, and otherwise—all increased by the fact that we have the largest educated Negro population in the world, and by the further fact that war conditions involving the United Nations are relating this country increasingly to Africa. . . .

RECOMMENDATIONS

(1) Political Conditions

That the goal of ultimate self-government should be definitely accepted in every colony, and that the controlling governments should show themselves both willing and eager to fit the African people for larger and larger participation in their own affairs both through "indirect rule" and through direct representation in government councils.

That every effort should be made to secure the best public opinion of the African population when any changes in governmental control or policy are contemplated.

That in every colony steps should be immediately taken to provide adequate native representation in the Legislative Council (or what corresponds to it), including some African members elected directly, or by qualified African electors, or by Tribal Councils, and that such membership should steadily increase with the years.

That immediate steps should be taken to throw open more positions in the Civil Service in every colony . . . making ability and not color the basis of choice—looking forward to the time when most Civil Service posts shall be held by Africans. . . .

That the Mandate ideal of the vital importance of native rights, welfare, and development should be applied in all African territory controlled by European powers and should be adopted by the independent African states.

That all European colonies in Africa should be willing . . . to submit to international inspection and report.

(2) Social-economic Conditions

That it is a matter of vital importance that all forms of racial discrimination based on the Nazi *"Herrenvolk"* idea should be eliminated, and that instead of looking upon different races as "superior" or "inferior" they should rather be considered as "advanced" or "retarded."

That all forms of industrial color-bars are as indefensible in Africa as they are in the United States, and that such as exist should be eliminated.

That the improvement of the economic status of native Africans is a matter of prime importance. . . .

That special attention should be given to the fundamental problem of land to make sure that Africans have adequate land of a good quality for all their needs. . . .

That everything possible be done through governmental controls to prevent the exploitation of the mineral, water,

plant, animal, and soil resources, by the adoption of a
sound conservation policy looking to the future as well
as the present of the inhabitants.

That, as agriculture is the primary occupation of the
overwhelming majority of Africans and largely the basis
of their economic security, everything possible should
be done to improve methods and practices of land management and of soil and crop conditions by education in
such fields as scientific agriculture, forestry, and irrigation.

That there is need in every colony of larger emphasis
on education directly related to the needs of the people,
and on training for effective leadership in education,
family life, medicine, agriculture, the ministry, public
life, economic and industrial planning, and other fields.

That social anthropology should be studied more,
thereby making more satisfactory the adjustments between
Western and African cultures.

That education should be based on the vernacular
supplemented in its later stages by the European language
of the nation concerned. . . .

That the health problems of Africa are exceptionally
serious and demand more attention through education
and health campaigns. . . .

That everything possible should be done . . . to prevent the exploitation of the African in industry; to give
him a larger wage; and to provide for him better housing
and recreational facilities. . . .

That in view of many serious defects in our treatment
of the Negro in the United States, we should approach
the problems of race relations in Africa with humility. . . .

(3) *American Relations with Africa*

That the Government of the United States, being already a party to many treaties and conventions dealing
particularly with Africa and the protection of its native
people, has assumed certain responsibilities which it
cannot escape; and should not only continue to participate
actively in international conferences but also in other
projects dealing with Africa.

That American financial and business interests with
investments in Africa should be specially careful to see

that African labor is treated fairly as to methods of employment, wages, living conditions, etc.

That the people of the United States should be willing, both through philanthropic and missionary societies, to devote more attention and more financial aid to Africa than in the past.

That our Government should stand ready to unite with other nations in some world organization (including a Mandate System) which will promote collective security and see to it that the provisions of the Atlantic Charter are duly implemented so as to protect the interests of Africans, who should be given some form of representation in connection with the Peace Conference. . . .

That the Government should consider establishing in the State Department a separate Division with most of its personnel having African experience, to deal with African-American affairs. . . .

— Reading No. 14 —

THE BRITISH LABOUR PARTY'S COLONIAL POLICY, 1942 [14]

Reform of colonial policy and emancipation of colonial peoples were constant themes of discussion during the war, especially in Britain and the United States. In the perfect world to be achieved by victory of the United Nations there was to be no imperialism, exploitation of native peoples, or colonial systems. The Labour Party issued the following statement on this problem.

[14] *Report of the 41st Annual Conference of the Labour Party,* cited in Louise W. Holborn, ed., *War and Peace Aims of the United Nations* (World Peace Foundation, Boston, 1943) p. 684. Reprinted by permission of World Peace Foundation.

This Conference considers that the time has arrived for a restatement of the principles of the Labour Party as applied to the government of the colonies and to the status of colonial peoples.

This should be a charter of freedom for colonial peoples abolishing all forms of imperialist exploitation and embodying the following main principles:

(1) All persons who are citizens of the colonial commonwealth should be considered to possess and be allowed to enjoy equality of political, economic, and social rights in the same way as the citizens of Great Britain.

(2) The status of colony should be abolished and there should be substituted for this that of States named according to the country in which they are situated and having an equal status with the other nations of the commonwealth.

(3) In all colonial areas there should be organised a system of democratic government, using the forms of indigenous institutions in order to enable the mass of people to enter upon self-government by the modification of existing forms of colonial administration in conformity with these principles.

(4) In all colonial areas, in Africa and elsewhere, where the primitive systems of communal land tenure exist, these systems should be maintained and land should be declared inalienable by private sale or purchase. All natural resources should be declared public property and be developed under public ownership.

(5) A commonwealth council of colonial peoples should be set up on which each former colonial state should be represented in accordance with the number of its population, but giving also special attention to the representation of national groups within each State.

BRITAIN'S POLITICAL PROGRAM FOR THE COLONIES, 1945 [15]

Speaking before an American audience in London in the closing months of World War II, Oliver Stanley, Secretary of State for the Colonies, paid particular attention to political aims for the colonial empire. This member of Winston Churchill's Government made a careful distinction between self-government and independence.

✓   ✓   ✓

We have the responsibility for 60 million people in the Colonial Empire. How is that responsibility to be discharged? There are some people on both sides of the Atlantic who are continually pressing for universal charters and for general schedules. Neither I am afraid is possible. The diversity among the various territories of the Colonial Empire, the difference in their present development and in their possibilities is so great that no common denominator can be found for the problem as a whole. All I can do is to state in general terms our aims and, in more detail, the ways in which under varying circumstances and in varying conditions we are proceeding to carry them out.

Politically our aim for the Colonial Empire can be briefly stated. It is that of the maximum practical self-government within the Empire at the earliest practicable time. I remember that before my first speech to an American audience, I was warned by earnest students of British publicity that the words self-government were suspect in America and that only the word independence would ring the bell. Well, I could not help it then and I cannot help it now. Anyone in my position has got to deal not

[15] Speech delivered by Rt. Hon. Oliver Stanley to the American Outpost, London, March 19, 1945. In *British Speeches of the Day* (London, 1945) pp. 318-320. Courtesy, British Information Services.

only with generous emotions but with hard realities, realities which may be very hard indeed to the people concerned if mistakes are made. It is self-government and not independence which I believe is to the real advantage of the Colonial territories, is in accordance with the wishes of the inhabitants themselves, and is in the best interest of the world as a whole. Let us just look at those three points.

First, with regard to the advantage of the territories. I feel there are many who fail to realize the composition and complexity of the Colonial Empire and the differences among its numerous territories. One or two of the colonies may be big but the majority of the 40 are comparatively small, and many of them are very small. Few of these territories are contiguous and most of them are widely separated. It may be that in some regions, despite the many practical obstacles, some of the separate colonies may in the future come together and so form areas sufficient in size and resources to enable us to contemplate ultimately for them the attainment of Dominion Status with all that Status implies. Even in these areas that possibility lies a long way ahead, but in others no such possibility exists, either now or in the future. St. Helena, the Falkland Isles, Seychelles, Aden—territories of that type, with no possibility of federation or amalgamation, no possibility by such means of increasing their size or their resources—how can we ever contemplate them being in a position where independence is a reality or if a reality could be an advantage? Nor do I believe that the goal of independence is in accordance with the wishes of the vast mass of inhabitants. Everywhere you find in varying forms and with varying intensity a desire for more control of their own affairs, a desire for a greater degree of self-government, a hope for the eventual attainment of complete self-government. But even among the most advanced political elements in the various territories, I find little or no desire to break the British connection. . . .

Finally, I do not believe that any splinterization of the British Colonial Empire would be in the interests of the world. Would it really be an advantage to create another 40 independent states, all small? Would the new machinery for world security, which is to be devised at San

Francisco next month, be made any the stronger by the substitution of these 40 states for a cohesive Empire able to act as a strategic whole? Would the economies of the new world be made any easier by 40 more separate divisions, 40 more political obstacles; would it free the flow of world trade?

And so it is advisedly that His Majesty's Government in their policy, and I in my speech today, use the term self-government in the British Empire and not that of independence. But in our desire for self-government we are sincere and, when we say that, we of all nations have the right to be taken at our word. We, after all, can point to the example of the great self-governing Dominions.

— Reading No. 16 —

THE BRAZZAVILLE CONFERENCE ON FRENCH COLONIAL POLICY, 1944 [16]

During World War II an important conference on colonial problems convened in Brazzaville, French Equatorial Africa. The Conference was attended by the Commissioner of Colonies M. Pleven and other high officials. A number of important recommendations were made dealing with political objectives, public education, labor and social-security policies, and medical facilities. The whole tenor of the conference was liberalization of the political philosophy of the French colonial empire and the more rapid advancement of its native populations.

[16] "French Colonial Policy in Africa," *Free France* (French Press and Information Service, New York) September 1944, pp. 8-9, and 12. Courtesy of the French Embassy.

✓   ✓   ✓

FIRST PART: POLITICAL ORGANIZATION

Political Organization of the French Colonies.—In
view of the complex problems involved, the representation of the colonies in a new French Constitution can be
studied adequately only by a commission of experts,
designated by the Government.

It appears, however, that these experts should take
into consideration the following principles to guide and
inspire their work:

1. It is desirable and even indispensable that the
colonies be represented in the future Assembly whose
task will be to draw up the new Constitution of France.

2. It is indispensable to ensure that the colonies be
represented in the central government in Metropolitan
France in a much more comprehensive and much more
effective manner than in the past.

3. Any project of reform which would aim merely at
an amelioration of the system of representation existing
on September 1, 1939 (colonial Deputies and Senators
in the French Parliament, Supreme Council of France
Overseas) appears *a priori* to be inadequate and sterile.

The same consideration would apply in particular to
an increase of the number of colonial Deputies and Senators in the French Metropolitan Parliament, as well as
to new seats which might be granted to colonies not
represented at present.

4. In any case, the new body to be created, Colonial
Parliament or, preferably Federal Assembly, must fulfill
the following purposes: Proclaim and guarantee the indissoluble unity of the French world—respect the regional
life and freedom of each of the territories members of the
bloc, composed of France and her colonies (or "French
Federation," if this term is accepted . . .). With this in
view it will be necessary to define, with great accuracy
and precision, the power reserved to the central authority
or federating body on the one hand, and those allotted
to the colonies, on the other hand.

5. The legislative regime of the colonies or, to use a
more specific terminology, the respective fields of the
laws, decrees and regulations, will be adequately determined only after the adoption of the decisions which will

establish on a new basis the powers of the central authority or federating body, and those of the various territories. Special emphasis will be laid on the fact that the colonies should gradually advance on the way leading from administrative decentralization to a status of political personality.

Internal Political Organization of the Colonies.—The chiefs of the colonies must exercise as much initiative as possible in their internal administration. With this in view, bodies of political expression must be created which will provide them with a perfectly balanced and legitimate system toward the European administration as well as toward the native population.

It is consequently suggested that the existing consultative bodies be abolished and replaced:

In the first place, by Councils of subdivision and Regional Councils, composed of native notables and availing themselves, whenever possible, of the framework provided by existing traditional institutions.

Secondly, by representative Assemblies, composed partly of Europeans, partly of natives.

The members of these bodies would be elected by universal suffrage wherever and whenever this would be practicable. . . .

The powers of the Councils of subdivision and the Regional Councils would be consultative; those of the Assemblies would be deliberative with regard to voting on the budget and establishing the programs for new works, and consultative with regard to all matters which are subject to the legislative and executive authority belonging to the Governor. In addition, Administrative Councils composed exclusively of functionaries, would assist the Governor with the application of the regulations.

SECOND PART: SOCIAL PROBLEMS

The Constitutive Elements of the Colonial Society: the Respective Place of the Europeans and of the Natives in Colonization.—Our entire colonial policy will be based upon the respect and the progress of the native society, and we shall have to accept fully and absolutely the demands and consequences implied by this principle. The natives may not be treated as devoid of human dignity, they can be subjected neither to eviction nor to

exploitation. However, the colonies are destined, by their
very nature, to be inhabited jointly by both Europeans
and natives. Although our policy must be subordinated
to the full development of the local races, we must also
give European activity the place to which it is entitled.

1. The prerequisite for the progress of the African
continent is the development of the native populations.
The activity of the Europeans and other non-Africans in
the colonial territories of Africa must conform to this
condition.

2. On the other hand, this progress of the African continent, as it is being contemplated, cannot be achieved
without the collaboration of non-African persons and
enterprises to a much greater extent and in greater proportion than at the present time. Consequently, all necessary talent, ability and services will be duly enlisted and
utilized. . . .

4. All the various trades must gradually be taken over
by the natives. The Governors-General and the Governors
of the territories shall establish, within a brief period, an
inventory of the enterprises which will be progressively
opened to the natives. It is particularly desirable in all
the African colonies that the responsibility of the executive branch of the administration be assumed, as rapidly
as possible, regardless of their personal status.

5. The education of the natives will be directed towards
this progressive accession to public office. Proper selection and adequate training will be the dominant tendency
in this field.

6. The necessity for training replacement personnel,
as well as the realization of the reforms recommended in
all domains by the French African Conference at Brazzaville, make it imperative to launch . . . large-scale re-
cruitment in order to meet the needs of the administrative
personnel as well as of the new colonial economy. . . .

THIRD PART: ECONOMIC QUESTIONS

The aim of our colonial economic policy must be to
develop production and to bring prosperity to the territories overseas, with a view to ensuring a better life for
the Africans by increasing their purchasing power and
by raising their standard of living. . . .

The industrialization of colonial territories is to be

encouraged. Industrialization should proceed methodically
. . . within the strict limits imposed by the application
of the plan for general production. With this in view, it
will be subjected to the regime of prior authorization and
of the control of its production by the public authorities.
Subject to these reservations, industrialization will be
effected by private enterprise. . . .

It is recommended that the quality of [agricultural]
products be improved by imposing high standards . . .
and by conducting scientific research work. . . . It is
proposed that an Institute of Agricultural Research of
French Africa be established in the near future. . . . A
School of Tropical Agriculture should be annexed to the
Institute, with a view to training experts in agriculture. . . .

It is recommended that the colonies submit within
four months a tentative estimate of the personnel, equipment, materials and supplies which will be necessary to
ensure, after the conclusion of hostilities, the functioning
of public services. . . .

— Reading No. 17 —

THE BRITISH COLONIAL EMPIRE AND COOPERATION WITH OTHER NATIONS[17]

*During World War II there was considerable discussion
of regionalism in the colonial empires, that is the creation
of regional commissions established to direct scientific
and medical research and economic development for a*

[17] *Britain Looks Ahead* (British Information Services, New
York, no date) III, 147. Courtesy, British Information
Services.

common colonial area, regardless of the nationality of the various colonies making up the area. Regionalism would thus constitute an important advance towards international cooperation in the development of backward colonial areas. The British position on this matter was explained in the House of Commons by the Secretary of State for the Colonies.

✓   ✓   ✓

The Prime Minister, in answer to a Question on the 17th of March, stated that, while His Majesty's Government were convinced that the administration of the British Colonies must continue to be the sole responsibility of Great Britain, the policy of His Majesty's Government was to work in close co-operation with neighboring and friendly nations. We realize that under present circumstances such co-operation is not only desirable but it is indeed essential.

Developments of modern transport and modern communications have brought close together vast areas which before were widely separated. Many of their problems today are common problems and can only be solved in co-operation, for problems of security, of transport, or economics, of health, etc., transcend the boundaries of political units. His Majesty's Government would therefore welcome the establishment of machinery which will enable such problems to be discussed and to be solved by common efforts. What they have in mind is the possibility of establishing Commissions for certain regions. These Commissions would comprise not only the States with Colonial Territories in the region, but also other States which have in the region a major strategic or economic interest. While each State would remain responsible for the administration of its own territory, such a Commission would provide effective and permanent machinery for consultation and collaboration so that the States concerned might work together to promote the well-being of the Colonial territories. An important consideration in designing the machinery of each Commission will be to give to the people of the Colonial territories in the region an opportunity to be associated with its work.

In this way it would be possible to have international

co-operation which consisted of something more than
theoretical discussion. . . . There are no fundamental
changes. We retain complete control of our administration. What we have in mind is merely the development
of the idea which led to the Anglo–United States Caribbean Commission.

— Reading No. 18 —

DRAFT TERMS OF TRUSTEESHIP FOR TANGANYIKA, 1946 [18]

*When the mandates of the League of Nations were trans-
ferred to the jurisdiction of the United Nations trusteeship
system, the former mandatories signed new agreements
governing their administration of the trust territories and
their responsibilities to the Trusteeship Council. Great
Britain, for example, accepted new terms regulating her
rule in Tanganyika.*

✓   ✓   ✓

WHEREAS the territory known as Tanganyika has been
administered in accordance with Article 22 of the Covenant of the League of Nations under a Mandate conferred on His Britannic Majesty; and

WHEREAS Article 75 of the United Nations Charter
signed at San Francisco on June 26th, 1945, provides for
the establishment of an International Trusteeship System
for the administration and supervision of such territories
as may be placed thereunder by subsequent individual
agreements; and

WHEREAS under Article 77 of the said Charter the

[18] *Trusteeship Territories in Africa under the United Kingdom
Mandate*, Cmd. 6935 (London, 1946) pp. 1–6. Reprinted by
permission of the Controller, Her Britannic Majesty's Stationery Office.

International Trusteeship System may be applied to territories now held under Mandate; and

WHEREAS His Majesty has indicated his desire to place Tanganyika under the said International Trusteeship System, and

WHEREAS . . . the placing of a territory under the International Trusteeship System is to be effected by means of a Trusteeship Agreement . . . agreed upon by the States concerned and approved by the United Nations: Now, THEREFORE, the General Assembly of the United Nations . . . having satisfied itself that the agreement of the States directly concerned, including the Mandatory Power, has been obtained in accordance with Article 79 of the said Charter, hereby resolves to approve the following terms of trusteeship for Tanganyika. . . .

ARTICLE 2. His Majesty is hereby designated as Administering Authority for Tanganyika, the responsibility for the administration of which will be undertaken by His Majesty's Government in the United Kingdom and Northern Ireland.

ARTICLE 3. The Administering Authority undertakes to administer Tanganyika in such a manner as to achieve the basic objectives of the International Trusteeship System. . . . The Administering Authority further undertakes to collaborate fully with the General Assembly of the United Nations and the Trusteeship Council in the discharge of all their functions . . . and to facilitate any periodic visits to Tanganyika which they may deem necessary, at times to be agreed upon with the Administering Authority.

ARTICLE 4. The Administering Authority shall be responsible (a) for the peace, order, good government and defence of Tanganyika, and (b) for ensuring that it shall play its part in the maintenance of international peace and security.

ARTICLE 5. For the above-mentioned purposes and for all purposes of this agreement . . . the Administering Authority:—

(a) shall have full powers of legislation, administration, and jurisdiction in Tanganyika . . .

(b) shall be entitled to constitute Tanganyika into a customs, fiscal or administrative union or federation with adjacent territories under his sovereignty or control, (*c*) and shall be entitled to establish naval, military and air bases, to erect fortifications, to station and employ his own forces in Tanganyika and to take all such other measures as are in his opinion necessary for the defence of Tanganyika. . . .

ARTICLE 6. The Administering Authority shall promote the development of political institutions suited to Tanganyika. To this end, the Administering Authority shall assure to the inhabitants of Tanganyika a progressively increasing share in the administration and other services of the territory; shall develop the participation of the inhabitants of Tanganyika in advisory and legislative bodies and in the government of the territory, both central and local, as may be appropriate to the particular circumstances of the territory and its peoples; and shall take all other appropriate measures with a view to the political advancement of the inhabitants of Tanganyika in accordance with Article 76(*b*) of the United Nation Charter. . . .

ARTICLE 8. In framing laws relating to the holding or transfer of land and natural resources, the Administering Authority shall take into consideration native laws and customs, and shall respect the rights and safeguard the interests . . . of the native population. No native land or natural resources may be transferred, except between natives, save with the previous consent of the competent public authority. No real rights over native land or natural resources in favour of non-natives may be created except with the same consent. . . .

ARTICLE 12. The Administering Authority shall, as may be appropriate to the circumstances of Tanganyika, continue and extend a general system of elementary education designed to abolish illiteracy and to facilitate the vocational and cultural advancement of the population, child and adult, and shall similarly provide such facilities as may prove desirable and practicable in the interests of the inhabitants or qualified students to receive secondary and higher education, including professional training. . . .

ARTICLE 14. Subject only to the requirements of public order, the Administering Authority shall guarantee to the inhabitants of Tanganyika freedom of speech, of the press, of assembly, and of petition. . . .

ARTICLE 16. The Administering Authority shall make
to the General Assembly of the United Nations an annual
report on the basis of a questionnaire drawn up by the
Trusteeship Council. . . . The Administering Authority
shall designate an accredited representative to be present
at the sessions of the Trusteeship Council at which the
reports of the Administering Authority with regard to
Tanganyika are considered. . . .

ARTICLE 19. If any dispute whatever shall arise between
the Administering Authority and another member of the
United Nations relating to the interpretation or application . . . of this agreement, if it cannot be settled by
negotiation or other means, shall be submitted to the
International Court of Justice provided for in Chapter
XIV of the United Nations Charter.

— Reading No. 19 —

BRITAIN'S ADMINISTRATION IN TANGANYIKA DEFENDED IN THE TRUSTEESHIP COUNCIL, 1948 [19]

*There has been some justification for the charge that the
Trusteeship Council has, at times, "degenerated into an
ideological forum." Some of its members have criticized
policies and administration in the trust territories, not
on the basis of protecting the welfare of native people
but rather as a means of embarrassing another great
power. The long arm of the cold war has often made*

[19] Cited in *British Information Services: Reference Division*
(New York, July 1948) pp. 13-14. Courtesy, British Information Services. Reprinted by permission of the Controller, Her Britannic Majesty's Stationery Office.

itself evident in the Trusteeship Council. The following are extracts from the reply of Britain's Sir Alan Burns to remarks by the Russian delegate on the administration of Tanganyika.

✦   ✦   ✦

I am always reluctant to import into our discussions anything which savours of an attack on any of my colleagues, and, I am always prepared to credit anyone, even when we hold different opinions, with honest and sincere convictions.

But, this must cut both ways and I am no believer in appeasement. I am not prepared tacitly to accept, as representative of the United Kingdom, the role of a target for all those who, for one reason or another, find it an amusing pastime to criticise my country and its administration of Tanganyika. I make no claim that our administration of this Trust Territory is perfect. Far from it. We have not the self-complacency of certain governments which seem to believe that they, and they alone, are gifted with all wisdom.

The United Kingdom in its administration of Trusteeship Territories has made mistakes, as is natural in any enterprise undertaken by fallible humans. We make no claim to Godlike perfection. But we do claim that we have done a great deal for the people of Tanganyika and other backward countries and that we have done at least as well as any other Power could have done, and better than most.

I would remind my colleagues that the principles of Trusteeship as embodied in the Charter are the same principles as those which have guided my country in its administration of dependent territories for a much longer period than this Council has existed, and that there is nothing in Trusteeship which has not been inherent in our policy for generations.

It is for this reason that I resent the suggestions or the innuendoes or the direct charges to which we have been treated, that the United Kingdom Government (and indeed other Administering Authorities) are not to be trusted, that the word of a self-advertising petitioner or any man with a grievance is to be accepted against a declared statement by the Administering Authority, in other words that all Administering Authorities are inherently wicked, and that it is only a select band of high-principled, pure-minded and truthful powers which can be trusted.

Much has been said of the petitions before the Council, and of the dissatisfaction of some people with the administration of Tanganyika. I wonder whether certain members of this Council have thought the matter out or whether they have leaped to conclusions. Can they not appreciate that it is the very freedom of speech, the liberty of conscience and opinion, which permits such expressions of discontent? In no country of the world are all the citizens satisfied with their Government, but there are many countries where the citizens dare not ventilate their grievances, where freedom of speech and freedom of the Press are denied, and where any expression of discontent would involve a speedy and terrible punishment. This is understandable, because there are countries whose governments dare not let the world know the conditions which exist. There is no such iron curtain shutting off Trusteeship Territories or British Colonies from public inspection. . . .

I yield place to no man in my desire to see the continued advancement of backward peoples and I assert that my Government is doing its best, and doing very well indeed, in carrying out the principles of the Charter and the terms of the Trusteeship Agreement. . . .

Irresponsible criticism of the Administering Authority does no good to the people of the Trust Territories and no credit to the Trusteeship Council.

KWAME NKRUMAH: FIRST PRIME MINISTER OF THE GOLD COAST, 1952 [20]

Kwame Nkrumah is rapidly becoming the idol and leader of millions of Africans, not only in his own native Gold Coast, but in territories extending as far south as the Union of South Africa. The following eulogistic sketch of the career of this leader appeared in one of the Gold Coast newspapers.

If Hamlet, who once told Horatio that there were more things in Heaven and earth than were dreamt of in his philosophy, were present at the Legislative Assembly when it was officially proclaimed that the Gold Coast Premier would be elected soon, he would have turned to his stooge and said with prophetic pride—"I told you so!"

For who would have guessed that the little boy who was born in a small village of Nzima in 1909, would one day, make history by becoming the Gold Coast's first premier?

Kwame was neither born great nor did he have greatness thrust upon him. He has achieved greatness through hard work, determination and that fixity and tenacity of purpose which characterises his personality.

His father was a goldsmith and his mother, a trader. But their lowly station in life, did not prevent them thinking and planning great things for their son. They worked hard and saved hard and when the time came for little Kwame to start his schooling they sent him to the Catholic Mission School at Nkroful.

[20] "Life Story of the Prime Minister," *The Gold Coast and the Constitution*. Pamphlet of the *Daily Graphic* (Accra, 1952) p. 3.

While there, he was an ambitious boy, devoted to his work and possessed of a high sense of responsibility. From Nkroful, he went to Sekondi where he continued his education at the Catholic Mission school. He showed signs of promise and his teachers decided that Kwame would do well in the teaching profession.

Thus when his school days were over, Kwame Nkrumah was appointed a teacher. . . . But Kwame's thirst for knowledge made him decide to further his education at Achimota College. There under the eye and instruction of Rev. A. G. Fraser, he made rapid progress and revealed convincing signs of his talent for public speaking.

It was at Achimota that Kwame Nkrumah met another student—Komla Agbeli Gbedemah—now minister of Commerce and Industry.

Even after he had completed his studies at Achimota, Kwame's insatiable thirst for knowledge made him restless. At last with only his fare and a little extra, he journeyed to the United States.

Life for him in America was not only financially precarious but hazardous in the extreme. Yet, he remained undaunted in the face of seemingly insurmountable difficulties.

The sun shone at last and the ambitious but financially handicapped young student . . . gained admission to Lincoln University [in] Pennsylvania. There again he met another Gold Coast student—Ako Adjei—now a barrister-at-law and Organising Secretary of the U.G.C.C. [a nationalist political organization].

He worked his way through Lincoln and graduated. . . . Still, he wanted to know more. His search after truth led him to pursue a theology course, at the end of which he obtained the B.D. degree. Kwame then took his Master of Arts degree and later he turned to science and graduated M. Sc.

Having acquired knowledge, he decided to pass on knowledge to others. He translated this dream into reality by becoming a lecturer in Lincoln University.

Ako Adjei was also a student and it was he who influenced Nkrumah to take up law. Nkrumah said good bye to America for another land—England. There he stayed in London.

But Nkrumah's stars shone darkly over him—his troubles started all over again. . . . He became stranded in London with no money. It was during this period that he met George Padmore and other Africans. They formed a political organisation of which Kwame became the first General Secretary.

During Kwame's absence from the Gold Coast a political organisation known as the United Gold Coast Convention had been formed in Accra. They needed a Secretary. Ako Adjei remembered his former colleague in Lincoln and Kwame received a letter offering him the post.

He accepted and returned home in November 1947 and took up his appointment. Apart from his secretarial duties, he travelled widely over the country talking to people. He was instrumental in establishing schools. Unfortunately there was a split in the U.G.C.C. which led Kwame to resign.

From that day forward, Kwame concentrated on political work. After the setting up of the Coussey Constitution Committee Kwame Nkrumah imbued the youth of the Gold Coast with an intensive and unabated desire for Self-government Now. On June 12, 1949, Kwame Nkrumah proclaimed at the Accra Arena the formation of the Convention People's Party (C.P.P.). Despite oppressive measures adopted by the Government, the C.P.P. remained undaunted.

Realising that the C.P.P. demands had not been met, Kwame Nkrumah declared Positive Action at the arena on January 8, 1950. Since that time, the political tension ran high until Kwame and some of his followers were arrested and imprisoned.

While in prison, the General Elections were held and Kwame's party (C.P.P.) topped the polls. Kwame was then released and invited by the Governor, Sir Charles Arden-Clarke, to become Leader of Government Business.

When the news of Kwame's success reached Dr. Horace Bond, President of Lincoln University, he invited Kwame to the United States. In June, 1951, Nkrumah received a warm welcome in New York and on June 6, 1951, the L.L.D. degree was conferred on him at Lincoln University. Leaving America he flew to

London, where he addressed public meetings and met British M.Ps.

On his return to the Gold Coast, he was given an enthusiastic welcome by his countrymen. As a politician he enjoys a unique popularity and travels widely in the country, addressing political meetings.

Formerly Leader of Government Business; now Prime Minister of the Gold Coast, Kwame Nkrumah is a man of great personal magnetism. . . . Careless about food and money, our Prime Minister is a dreamer. He has visions of a self-governing Ghana and he has dedicated his life to the task of liberating Ghana from Imperialist domination. . . .

The elevation of an African to the Office of Premiership within the Commonwealth is a challenge to Malan's racial creed. Whether Dr. Malan likes it or not, from now on an African Prime Minister will sit with other Dominion Prime Ministers in a Commonwealth Conference. Thus the elevation of Kwame Nkrumah means the decline and fall of Malan's Herrenvolk institution.

— Reading No. 21 —

A BRITISH COLONIAL GOVERNOR WARNS AGAINST PREMATURE SELF-GOVERNMENT, 1947 [21]

The British Governor of Nigeria, Sir Arthur Richards, addressing the legislative council meeting for the first time under the new constitution, urged its members to appreciate the complexity of democratic government and

[21] Cited in Joan Wheare, *The Nigerian Legislative Council* (Faber & Faber, Ltd., London, 1949) pp. 250-252. Reprinted by permission of Faber & Faber, Ltd.

the necessity for more training on the part of the various peoples of Nigeria before complete self-rule was achieved.

✓   ✓   ✓

I am assuming that you are all familiar with the analysis which I made . . . of our problems, and the sketch of a new Constitution which would contain within itself the living possibilities of expansion and development. My object was to avoid rigidity and to make agreed change possible and easy to achieve. I did not expect or even wish to avoid criticism. Opinions differ so widely about the pace at which growing responsibilities can be absorbed. I agree that some risks must be taken in order to achieve progress, but I would also emphasize the wisdom of avoiding undue haste. By undue haste I mean irresponsible haste. The fate of over twenty-two million people is at stake. It has been well said that political independence is not an easy thing to bear and without a strong sense of citizenship and a power of economic resistance independence would prove a bane to the people at large. I am aware that a group of Nigerians claim immediate self-government. It is perhaps a natural claim to make for the impatient patriot who has had access to Western education and political thought. But they are as yet untested in positions of responsibility and to transfer all political authority suddenly to their untried hands would be but a sham democracy. The desire to drive a passenger bus does not necessarily breed the ability to do so. That has to be tested by practice under qualified control. At present you have in Nigeria a large measure of local self-government, but in the main structure of government you have a corps of advisory and executive Europeans whose purpose is to carry on the work of the country, and to help to train the Africans who will ultimately take their place. It is not enough to have men capable of doing this job or that, you need to foster institutions and a system of government which will place ultimate control in the hands of the adult citizens of the country and will provide those citizens with a means of expressing their views, and of educating themselves to express them and so of choosing their own government. Democracy means just that. No man or group of men can stand the temptations of uncontrolled power. The present system of government in this country consists of a series of checks and balances in which your Chiefs and people and various Councils participate with a certain ultimate control exercised by this Council and by His Majesty's Secretary of State for the Colonies. I regard the Administrative Service as the scaffolding which supports those working on a new building in process of erection until the building is ready to stand alone and the scaffolding can be removed.

May I quote to you the words of an American President uttered a generation ago: "The ability of a people to govern themselves is not easily attained. History is filled with the failures of popular government. It cannot be learned from books; it is not a matter of eloquent phrases. Liberty, freedom, independence are not mere words, the repetition of which brings fulfilment. They demand long, arduous, self-sacrificing preparation. Education, knowledge, experience, sound public opinion, intelligent participation by the great body of the people —these things are essential. The degree in which they are possessed determines the capability of a people to govern themselves." I do not think that Nigeria is yet a sufficiently coherent whole, whether in the political, social or economic sphere, to be capable of immediate and full self-government. The new Constitution is designed to encourage the sense of unified interest beyond the realm of tribal jealousies, and to provide the training for ever swifter advances towards self-government. May I re-echo the words of the President whom I have just quoted and say in frankness and friendliness that demonstration of the ability to carry on successfully the large powers of government already possessed would be far more convincing than continued agitation for complete independence. I want this Constitution to work successfully as an advance to greater responsibilities, which carries within itself the seeds of further progress, so that when the time comes the assumption of full power will have come to pass unchallenged, because a system of true representation of the people will have developed.

— Reading No. 22 —

THE NATURE AND THE ORIGINS OF THE MAU MAU IN KENYA[22]

Since 1952 the once tranquil land of the colony of Kenya has been disfigured by terror and murder. The lonely farms of the European settlers have been in constant fear of attack by Mau Mau raiders; and there have been many instances where whole European families have been wiped out. The exact causes for this terroristic activity of the Kikuyu tribe have been the cause of much discussion and controversy. The following statement seeks to present the fundamental elements behind the Mau Mau movement.

✓   ✓   ✓

The Government and people of Kenya are faced with a challenge to law, order and progress not from the Africans of Kenya as a whole, but from the Mau Mau, an organisation within one tribe, the Kikuyu, but strongly opposed by a large and growing proportion of the Kikuyu themselves. The first duty of the Government is to restore law and order, to apprehend and punish those guilty of the many and bestial crimes committed by the Mau Mau against Africans and others alike, and of organising the Mau Mau movement itself. Only then can progress towards political advancement and interracial cooperation be resumed.

The exact nature and origin of the Mau Mau movement are in some respects obscure. It is almost entirely a Kikuyu movement, and it appears to derive from certain peculiarities of the Kikuyu tradition and tribal organisation. This tradition is permeated with witch-

[22] *Kenya—The Mau Mau: A Background Note Issued by the Information Office, British Embassy* (Washington, 1952). Courtesy, British Information Services.

craft, which has always played a very important part in Kikuyu tribal customs, particularly in relation to the use of land. It has indeed been suggested that the Mau Mau movement represents, in part, a last effort by witch-doctors to retain their influence in face of the advance of education and civilisation. Furthermore, traditionally, tribal custom in the Kikuyu has forbidden military age-groups to engage in most forms of agriculture, these being left to women, children and old men.

The East African tribes have adapted themselves with varying degrees of success to the disappearance of tribal warfare as a normal practice, but in none has difficulty with the younger age groups been quite as acute as among the Kikuyu. This is partly due to the fact that the tribe has been particularly affected by the urban influence of Nairobi, where young men of the Kikuyu have drifted in considerable numbers. The problem of young and able-bodied men with insufficient socially sanctioned employment, subject to the disturbing influence of an urban civilisation and meretricious attractions of urban life, is one to which an answer is still being sought in many parts of the world. Among other things, it means that there is a large number of able-bodied men living in circumstances which make them ripe for crime.

These factors have been recognised and skilfully exploited by ambitious men, and for that reason the Government of Kenya is bound to root out ringleaders who have sought to turn the situation to their own personal advantage. It is noteworthy, again, that similar conditions do not obtain among other tribes, many of whom are in fact hostile to the Kikuyu, believing that the Mau Mau and its leaders aim not at African but Kikuyu dominance in Kenya. There is in fact in the Mau Mau a strong element of exclusive nationalism, based not on racial and national pride, but on envy and hate. This basis is demonstrated in the extreme ruthlessness sometimes shown towards Kikuyu themselves, who have been by far the most numerous victims of the Mau Mau.

There is no evidence that communism or Communist agents have had any direct or indirect part in the organisation or direction of the Mau Mau itself, or its activities. Jomo Kenyatta, its leader, visited Moscow some time before 1947. But there is no evidence of Communist technique in the organisation and activities of the movement, which are in an African idiom. . . .

One of the most obvious facets of the Mau Mau organisation is that it is violently anti-European, and much play is made in its propaganda with the existence of the so-called "White Highlands." The main problem confronting African farmers is in fact not so much an absolute shortage of land (much of the land in the Reserves is not being cultivated to full productivity) but the necessity of carrying out the difficult transfer from a primitive shifting subsistence agriculture to a much more productive system of fixed agriculture, which is essential if higher standards of living are to be achieved. To this end, $8.4 million have been allocated by the Government of Kenya in a 10-Year Plan for African settlement and the reconditioning of African lands. . . . Great efforts have been made by the Government to teach new methods and many Africans have taken full advantage of them, not only as regards food crops for consumption but also as regards export crops, such as tea, coffee, and pyrethrum. . . . Advances have taken place in the Kikuyu reserve as elsewhere, but the Mau Mau leaders have among other things stirred up opposition to improved agriculture and have gone so far as to incite people to destroy contour terraces and other improvement works. In this respect the Mau Mau movement resembles that of the loom-breakers at the time of the Industrial Revolution in England, and stands in the way of the economic advance of the Kikuyu people— and of all Africans in Kenya.

— Reading No. 23 —

THE PSYCHOLOGICAL ASPECTS OF THE MAU MAU'S KILLING OATH, 1954 [23]

[23] *Report by the Parliamentary Delegation to Kenya,* Cmd. 9081 (London, 1954) pp. 11-12. Reprinted by permission of the Controller, Her Britannic Majesty's Stationery Office.

*A Czech medical student, acquainted with the psycho-
logical problems of freed war prisoners, displaced persons, and the torture techniques of the secret police in
postwar Europe, after visiting Kenya and studying the
Mau Mau, prepared a report for a British Parliamentary
delegation that visited Kenya in 1953. An extract from
this report is cited by the delegation in its findings presented to the British Colonial Secretary.*

      ✓   ✓   ✓

A very clever man, a man knowing the psychology of
his peoples, their superstitions, their fear of witchcraft,
must have made the plan. The Killing Oath was the
answer. A similar Oath was used in the times before the
Mau Mau to catch thieves, for instance; all stolen
property returned, the Oath was nullified. The present
Oath is "killing both ways." It forces a man or woman
to kill when called upon to do so, or it kills the man or
woman upon breaking the Oath, whether force was used
in the administration or whether taken willingly. It was
essential to create a new society divorced from all that
was once holy to the Kikuyu. In every primitive community certain stabilising factors were necessary to an
orderly disciplined life. The Oath had to cut across
everything in order to create the Mau Mau Society. The
ceremonies were devised to break every tribal taboo—
which the elder Kikuyu believed would cause his death,
and from which there was no Cleansing Ceremony—and
every modern taboo imposed by the Christian way of
life, to embrace the young modern thinking Kikuyu. The
higher the Oath the more outlawed the individual became. The effect on the mind of a primitive people was
overwhelming and is most difficult to assess by an outsider.

It has been possible to transform the human being into
a new frame of mind unknown and never met by me
before. After having taken three or more oaths the personality of the Oath-taker has changed. It is not in-
sanity, even if it appears as such, but the person is not
sane in the normal sense of the word. These people do
not hesitate or think any more. They murder but not
for the sake of furthering a cause, they just kill on being instructed to kill, their own mother, their own baby.

They admit themselves that they are no good to anybody any more after taking what they call a frightful Oath. Death for them means only deliverance, they told me. . . . Imagine a quite intelligent young African, an African you have known for years, made, with three Oaths, in three months, into a different human being. An intelligent European just cannot grasp, cannot understand what happens. I have asked loyal Africans whether they can explain. Even they cannot give a satisfactory explanation of this mutational phenomenon.

— Reading No. 24 —

THE INDIAN COMMUNITY IN EAST AFRICA, 1929 [24]

There has been considerable controversy over the place of the Indian in the economic and political life of East Africa. There are some who believe that he will be displaced eventually by the African as the latter is educated to perform the trade and skilled-artisan functions now in the hands of Indians. On the other hand, there are observers who, seeing overcrowded India across the Indian Ocean, prophesy that this subcontinent's logical area for mass emigration and expansion must be East Africa. The following extract from a British official report examines the status and prospects of the Indian community.

✓   ✓   ✓

The connection of India with the East Coast of Africa is of very long standing. Several references in the Puranas show that the ancient Hindus had a fairly

[24] *Report of the Commission on Closer Union of the Dependencies,* Cmd. 3234 (London, 1929) pp. 26-30. Reprinted by permission of the Controller, Her Britannic Majesty's Stationery Office.

accurate idea of the locality and its peoples. The voyages of Vasco da Gama at the end of the 15th century opened up direct sea communication between the two countries and stimulated trade. . . . In 1811 [it was] reported that there was a considerable interchange of goods between Zanzibar and various ports on the Bombay coast. . . .

A new Indian element was introduced in 1895 when the British Government took over the direct administration of the territory previously assigned under charter to the Imperial British East Africa Company, and decided to construct the Kenya-Uganda Railway. At first an attempt was made to carry out the work by native labour, but it was found impossible to obtain a sufficiently large or continuous supply, and an appeal was therefore made to the Government of India for assistance. Eventually the work was completed by Indian labour from the Punjab.

The majority of the Indian labourers returned to India on completing their term of service on the railway, but a certain number remained. A few settled on the land, as market gardeners near the coast ports and Nairobi, or as farmers at Kibos near Kisumu, where they or their successors are growing sugar and other crops on a considerable scale. Others found work as artisans, chiefly as carpenters or engineers, and still more of them became petty traders and money-lenders. The railway itself found it necessary to retain the services of a considerable number, both for clerical work and for skilled and unskilled labour. The clerical staff was almost entirely Indian, chiefly Goanese, and the overseers of the labourers were about half Indians and half Europeans. The unskilled Indian labour has since been replaced by native labour and in recent years the supply of skilled African labour has greatly increased and is being utilised to a growing extent in place of the more expensive Indian artisan.

There can be no doubt that in the past the Indian community has played a useful, and in fact an indispensable, part in the development of these territories. Apart from the construction of the Kenya-Uganda Railway, the services of Indian artisans and mechanics have been widely used by the public at large on works for which European agency would have been too costly and which the native is not yet fitted to perform. The Indian trader has been a potent factor in the process of civilising the African. The *"dukawala,"* or petty shop-keeper, has carried his wares far and wide into remote native areas, and introduced the products of European industry among the most primitive tribes. By increasing their wants he has created an incentive to effort and thus sown the first seeds of economic progress. The Indian dealer has performed another useful function in marketing the products of native agriculture. For instance, the greater part of the valuable cotton crop in Uganda is handled by Indian buyers. . . . We have heard complaints of unfair dealings by Indian traders, both as buyers and sellers, low prices secured by the former and exorbitant prices charged by the latter, and false measures used by both. Such charges are brought against middlemen all the world over, and no doubt the ignorance of the African offers special opportunities to the unscrupulous. But the middleman generally survives as a necessary link in the chain of distribution, and it must be recognized that the Indian middlemen are doing useful work for which no other agency is at present available. The European cannot afford to trade on the small scale with the small margins on which the Indian subsists and the African generally is not yet sufficiently advanced to do so.

It will thus be seen that in the economic organisation of the Eastern African territories the Indian, both as trader and as artisan, occupies an intermediate position between the European and the African. . . . As regards artisans and mechanics, there is already a certain amount of active competition between the European and the Indian, as for instance in motor driving and in various branches of engineering, and that competition will increase wherever white settlement establishes itself on a permanent basis. . . . [The Indian] is threatened on the other flank by the increasing efficiency of cheap African labour. The Bantu has undoubted capacity for mechanical work of a certain type. . . . They appear, however, to prefer repetitive tasks where no initiative is required, and where the workman is little more than a cog in the machine. . . . On the whole it appears improbable that the Indian artisan, in the near future at any rate, will be wholly squeezed out between the European and the African, though the competition from both sides makes it unlikely that there will be any substantial increase in numbers.

With regard to retail trade European competition is limited at present to comparatively large shops, mostly in towns. The main rival that the small Indian shopkeeper will have to face in the future is the African. . . . The only other industry which has been suggested as likely to lead to a large influx of Indian immigrants is agriculture. . . . The truth seems to be that there is no real demand at present for Indian settlement in these areas. Nor is there any likelihood of agricultural settlement from India on a large scale. . . .

Our general conclusions from the above considerations is that economic forces are already operating as a check on Indian immigration and are likely to operate still more strongly in the future.

— Reading No. 25 —

EXTRACTS FROM THE RHODESIA-NYASALAND ROYAL COMMISSION REPORT, 1939 [25]

In November 1937 a Royal commission was appointed by the British Government to study amalgamation in British Central Africa. In 1938 some three months were spent in the territories traveling and hearing evidence. The following are extracts from the Commission's report.

[25] *Rhodesia-Nyasaland Royal Commission Report,* Cmd. 5949 (London, 1939) pp. 214, 216, 217-218. Reprinted by permission of the Controller, Her Britannic Majesty's Stationery Office.

For our part we believe that Southern Rhodesia, Northern Rhodesia, and Nyasaland will become more and more closely interdependent in all their activities, and that identity of interests will lead them sooner or later to political unity. . . .

[But] we feel that, in view of the special responsibility of Your Majesty's Government . . . there should before amalgamation can be contemplated as a practical and salutary development, be a greater degree of certainty than there is at present that Southern Rhodesia's recently initiated policy of Parallel Development . . . will in the long run prove to be in the best interests of the natives, and will afford them full opportunity of advancement in those fields of activity for which they are fitted, and at the same time open up the prospect of a reasonably rapid improvement in their economic and cultural status.

In Northern Rhodesia one of the main reasons for the advocacy of amalgamation by many Europeans was the prospect thereby opened up of speedy emancipation from "Colonial Office control." Insufficient consideration appears to have been given to the dominant question of the position of the native consequent upon any such changes, or to the problem of the unification or the assimilation of the divergent native policies at present being pursued.

The striking unanimity, in the Northern Territories, of the native opposition to amalgamation, based mainly on dislike for some features of the native policy of Southern Rhodesia, and the anxiety of the natives in Northern Rhodesia and Nyasaland lest there should be any change in the system under which they regard themselves as enjoying the direct protection of Your Majesty, are factors which cannot in our judgment be ignored.

— Reading No. 26 —

OPPOSITION OF NATIVE AFRICANS TO AMALGAMATION OF BRITISH CENTRAL AFRICAN TERRITORIES, 1943 [26]

The African population of Nyasaland and Northern Rhodesia was strongly opposed to union with Southern Rhodesia when the idea was first strongly supported in the 1930's. The following is a statement made in 1943 by an African schoolmaster in a native urban advisory council in Northern Rhodesia.

✓   ✓   ✓

. . . Now that this dreaded question has been discussed at the recent sitting of the Legislative Council it becomes necessary for the African to speak on the subject once more.

I said dreaded question. The Africans in this country dread the very idea of amalgamating this country with Southern Rhodesia. When the Royal Commission came to enquire about the relationships and possibilities of amalgamating the two Rhodesias and Nyasaland, very strong and reasonable objections were pronounced by the Africans of this country. Many letters too of objections were printed in the *Bantu Mirror*. These strong and reasonable objections have remained unchanged in the minds of Africans.

I may throw light on the question if I mention some of the strongest and most reasonable objections which

[26] Statement made in Regional Council: Western Province of Northern Rhodesia. Chairman's Report of Frst Meeting, December 20, 1943. Cited in J. W. Davidson, *The Northern Rhodesian Legislative Council* (Faber & Faber, Ltd., London, 1947) pp. 113-114. Reprinted by permission of Faber & Faber, Ltd.

were given to the Royal Commissioner by the Africans of this country—and these are:

(a) The land question in Southern Rhodesia is very acute. There are thousands of landless Africans who are living as squatters in their native land, on lands owned by the white settlers. These landless Africans will no doubt, if amalgamation were to be enforced, move into Northern Rhodesia and aggravate our land problem here.

(b) The South African Native Policy of economic and political discrimination and racial segregation is adopted as the official Native Policy of the Southern Rhodesia Government. The Prime Minister of Southern Rhodesia has made it clear to everybody that his country is a white man's country and that the black man shall always remain a servant of the white man, if not a slave. On the other hand the Northern Rhodesia Government had from the time it took over from the South African Chartered Company given the African interests a very prominent place. The African Chieftainships have grown and are being given wider powers in the administration of the people. Educated Africans play an important part in the Civil Service, the same, of course, applies to the Mining and Commercial companies. State expenses on Education and Health are not determined on a racial basis as is the case in Southern Rhodesia. Will the Prime Minister of Southern Rhodesia drop down his Native Policy and follow suit with that of Northern Rhodesia and Nyasaland?

If His Majesty's Government would sign an agreement (which must have the approval of the Africans) with Southern Rhodesia Government that the now existing Native Policy in Northern Rhodesia will not be altered, then the Africans in this country will speak in favour of the question. If no agreement of the kind is made and the Dominions Office decided to hand over Northern Rhodesia and Nyasaland to Sir Godfrey Huggins, the black peoples in the entire British East Africa will fast lose confidence in the British Imperial Government.

I may add that those traders and capitalists who find it difficult to do their business in Northern Rhodesia . . . should be told to pack and go elsewhere and leave us here in peace.

BRITISH PLEDGES AND THE SOUTH AFRICAN PROTECTORATES, 1909 [27]

In the debate in the British House of Lords on the bill establishing a Union of South Africa, the Earl of Crewe defined the British Government's responsibility toward the three protectorates—Bechuanaland, Swaziland, and Basutoland. During the past twenty-five years the desire of the South African Government to annex these protectorates and the reluctance of Great Britain to place their inhabitants under the Union's native policy have constituted a major issue between the two governments.

↗   ↗   ↗

That brings me to Clause 151 of the Bill, the clause which enables what are known as the Protectorates possibly at some future time to be transferred to the care of the Union under regulations provided for in a Schedule. The South African Union finds itself in a unique position—a different position from that of any other part of the Empire. Not only has it got a vast native population within its borders, but just outside its borders, and in one case entirely surrounded by the Union itself, there are whole countries, hitherto directly administered by the Crown, in some cases almost entirely inhabited by natives and carried on under the immemorial tribal system. These Protectorates have been under our direct administration, and towards them we feel that we have a very solemn duty indeed. They were, speaking generally, not conquered by the arms of Great Britain, but came voluntarily under our control. They feel a profound confidence in the British Government, a confidence which has largely been inspired by able men who from time to time have administered them, and, when the

[27] *Debates of the House of Lords,* July 27, 1909.

question of [South African] union became urgent, we had to consider what was the best course to take in view of our honourable obligations towards the Protectorates. We felt bound to regard ourselves as trustees for these bodies of natives, and considering that it does not do for a trustee to hand over his trust to another man, however great his personal confidence may be in him, without a guarantee that the trust itself will be taken over, we decided to ask South Africa to accept the provisions embodied in the Schedule. Some opposition has been raised to the Schedule from two very different quarters. Some think that under no circumstances ought the native Protectorates to be handed over to the Union at all.

Here I may say that we have no desire, we are in no hurry, to hand over these areas to anyone. They are contented . . . in fact, they have expressed themselves as averse to passing from under the direct administration of the Crown. . . . It does not seem conceivable (however) that for an indefinite future these areas should remain administered from here and that the new South African Union should have no lot or part in their administration. . . . What weighs with me as much as anything is that the natives themselves are not anxious to be transferred, but, admitting that they may be some day transferred, actively desire the incorporation of a charter such as this in the Act itself. To me those reasons seem conclusive for the existence of this somewhat unusual form of provision in the form of a Schedule.

. . . The Schedule provides against the alienation of native lands, which involves the prohibition of indiscriminate prospecting; it provides against the supply of liquor to natives; and it provides that the restrictions which may exist in any of these territories on the supply of liquor to other than natives shall not be weakened if the territories are taken over. It also provides for the permanence of the native assemblies which have existed heretofore. These are the securities which we conceive to be given by the Schedule. . . . I believe it has been frankly accepted by South Africa.

THE SOUTH AFRICAN NATIONAL- IST PARTY DEFINES ITS RACIAL POLICY, 1948 [28]

In the spring of 1948, prior to a general election, Dr. Malan, then the prime minister, and Mr. Strijdom, who was later to succeed his chief as head of the government, made several statements laying down the Nationalist Party's stand on basic issues of racial policy.

✦ ✦ ✦

Referring to the stand taken by a member of the opposition United Party, Mr. Strijdom declared: The Hon. Minister of Mines [Mr. J. H. Hofmeyr] rejects with contempt the principles of the white man's domination. He dismisses with scorn the Herrenvolk idea. . . . Are we ruling South Africa as a result of his stupid leadership idea? No, we are ruling South Africa today because the legislation placed the power in our hands and not in the hands of his friends. . . . But he does not want to rule the country by power. Our policy is that the Europeans must stand their ground and must remain Baas [master] in South Africa. If we reject the Herrenvolk idea and the principle that the white man cannot remain Baas, if the franchise is to be extended to the non-Europeans, and if the non-Europeans are given representation and the vote and . . . are developed on the same basis as the Europeans, how can the Europeans remain Baas? Our view is that in every sphere the European must retain the right to rule the country and to keep it a white man's country.

Dr. Malan made his position clear in the following statement: Give the non-Europeans numerical strength;

[28] *Treatment of Indians in South Africa.* Pamphlet issued by the Government of India Information Services (Washington, no date) pp. 4, 5, 7.

give them social security; give them the right to organise in the field of labour; give them political equality and give them arms, and then there is only one ultimate result and that is the non-European will govern the country and the European will have to leave it.

Dr. Malan's views on the Indian minority in South Africa were set out thus: The Party hold the view that Indians are a foreign and outlandish element which is unassimilable. They can never become part of the country and must therefore be treated as an immigrant community. The Party accepts as a basis of its policy the repatriation of as many Indians as possible and proposes a proper investigation into the practicability of such a policy on a large scale in cooperation with India and other countries.

— Reading No. 29 —

SOUTH AFRICA'S *APARTHEID* POLICY DEFENDED, 1953[29]

Speaking before the Rotary Club in London, England, on August 19, 1953, Dr. A. L. Geyer, High Commissioner of the Union of South Africa in the United Kingdom, explained why his government led by Dr. Malan believes that apartheid is the best policy for both races, black and white, in South Africa.

ィ   ィ   ィ

As one of the aftermaths of the last war, many people seem to suffer from a neurotic guilt-complex with regard to colonies. This has led to a strident denunciation of the Black African's wrongs, real or imaginary, under the white man's rule in Africa. It is a denunciation, so shrill

[29] Press release of Union of South Africa Government Information Office, New York, 1953.

and emotional, that the vast debt owed by Black Africa to those same white men is lost sight of (and, incidentally, the Black African is encouraged to forget that debt). Confining myself to that area of which I know at least a very little, Africa south of the Equator, I shall say this without fear or reasonable contradiction: Every millemetre of progress in all that vast area is due entirely to the White Man.

You are familiar with the cry that came floating over the ocean from the West, a cry that "colonialism" is outmoded and pernicious, a cry that is being vociferously echoed by a certain gentleman in the East. [This refers to Jawaharlal Nehru, Prime Minister of India.]

May I point out that African colonies are of comparatively recent date. Before that time Black Africa did have independence for a thousand years and more—and what did she make of it? One problem, I admit, she did solve most effectively. There was no over-population. Interminable savage inter-tribal wars, witchcraft, disease, famine, and even cannibalism saw to that.

Let me turn to my subject, to that part of Africa, South of the Sahara, which, historically, is not part of Black Africa at all—my own country. Its position is unique in Africa as its racial problem is unique in the world.

1. South Africa is no more the orignial home of its black Africans, the Bantu, than it is of its white Africans. Both races went there as colonists and, what is more, as practically contemporary colonists. In some parts the Bantu arrived first, in other parts the Europeans were the first comers.

2. South Africa contains the only independent white nation in all Africa—a South African nation which has no other homeland to which it could retreat; a nation which has created a highly developed modern state, and which occupies a position of inestimable importance.

3. South Africa is the only independent country in the world in which white people are outnumbered by black people. Including all coloured races or peoples, the proportion in Brazil is 20 to 1. In South Africa it is 1 to 4.

Numbers, however, by no means constitute the only difference. The ancestors of the American Negroes were taken there as slaves 200 years ago. They were up-rooted from their tribal homes and their tribal associa-tions. Right from the beginning they were brought into close and continuous contact with white people. The result has been that the North American Negroes, for example, are no longer Africans. They are Americans, speaking the language of North America and following the American way of life.

Yet the United States has by no means solved its Negro problem. And who will say that in the United States there is no racial discrimination, sometimes very considerable racial discrimination. Now take the case of our black population. Our Bantu are still overwhelm-ingly tribal, and still speak half-a-dozen Bantu languages. Almost half of them still live permanently on their ancestral tribal lands, largely still following their tribal way of life. It is, after all, only about 100 years ago that the first of these warlike tribes were brought under European rule and very indirect rule at that.

When one remembers all this, when one remembers that . . . at the turn of the century the country was devastated in the course of a three years' war between Great Britain and the Republics; and when one remem-bers that the 43-year-old Union of South Africa has been involved in two world wars, then we can justly claim that the progress made in uplifting our primitive Bantu has been remarkable indeed.

There are over 800,000 Bantu children at school. Last year we spent about 8 million pounds on this education, compared with 3.6 million pounds when the Malan Government came into power five years ago. There are:

2 Agricultural Colleges
28 teaching hospitals for the training of nurses
33 Training Colleges for teachers
3 schools for the deaf, and
4 schools for the blind

There is a Bantu university college, affiliated to one of our universities. Another university has two separate sections, one for white and the other for coloured stu-dents, both served by the same staff. There is a Medical School, attached to the Natal University, for coloured students. The plain fact is that South Africa is doing more for its Bantu than is being done for Black Africans anywhere else in Africa; more, too, than is being done for the illiterate, poverty stricken, sometimes Untouchable, masses of those countries that denounce us most vehemently in the United Nations. . . .

This brings me to the question of the future. To me there seems to be two possible lines of development: *Apartheid* or Partnership. Partnership means cooperation of the individual citizens within a single community, irrespective of race. . . . [It] demands that there shall be no discrimination whatsoever in trade and industry, in the professions and the Public Service. There, whether a man is black or a white African, must according to this policy be as irrelevant as whether in London a man is a Scotsman or an Englishman. I take it that Partnership must also aim at the eventual disappearance of all social segregation based on race. This policy of Partnership admittedly does not envisage immediate adult suffrage. Obviously, however, the loading of the franchise in order to exclude the great majority of the Bantu could be no more than a temporary expedient. . . . [In effect] "there must one day be black domination, in the sense that power must pass to the immense African majority." Need I say more to show that this policy of Partnership could, in South Africa, only mean the eventual disappearance of the white South African nation? And will you be greatly surprised if I tell you that this white nation is not prepared to commit national suicide, not even by slow poisoning?

The only alternative is a policy of *apartheid,* the policy of separate development. The germ of this policy is inherent in almost all of our history, implanted there by the force of circumstances. . . . *Apartheid* is a policy of self-preservation. We make no apology for possessing that very natural urge. But it is more than that. It is an attempt at self-preservation in a manner that will also enable the Bantu to develop fully as a separate people.

We believe that, for a long time to come, political power will have to remain with the whites, also in the interest of our still very immature Bantu. But we believe also, in the words of a statement by the Dutch Reformed Church in 1950, a Church that favours *apartheid,* that "no people in the world worth their salt, would be content indefinitely with no say or only indirect say in the affairs of the State or in the country's socio-economic organisation in which decisions are taken about their interests and their future."

The immediate aim is, therefore, to keep the races outside the Bantu areas apart as far as possible, to continue the process of improving the conditions and standards of living of the Bantu, and to give them greater responsibility for their own local affairs. At the same time the long-range aim is to develop the Bantu areas both agriculturally and industrially, with the object of making these areas in every sense the national home of the Bantu—areas in which their interests are paramount, in which to an ever greater degree all professional and other positions are to be occupied by them, and in which they are to receive progressively more and more autonomy.

Frankly the obstacles in the way of this policy are enormous. We have followed a policy of laissez-faire for far too long. The Bantu areas, although consisting of 50,000 square miles of the best land in South Africa, are too small. The economic integration of the Bantu as the result of industrial development makes such a policy extremely difficult of execution. It is, moreover, a policy that demands heavy sacrifices from the whites, and democracies in peacetime are notoriously loath to make sacrifices for the benefit of future generations.

Now it is often stated that it is an impracticable policy. I don't agree. But let us, for argument's sake, admit that it may be impracticable. On the other hand, I firmly believe that the alternative policy of Partnership cannot possibly create a single harmonious, multi-racial society under South African conditions. And certainly, there is as much chance of the South African electorate—who are the Whites remember—accepting this policy of Partnership as there is of the United Kingdom becoming a Soviet Republic within a year. . . .

I am not suggesting that no one outside South Africa should discuss our problem. On the contrary, constructive, objective discussion, based on the full facts of the South African situation could be most helpful. But . . . in the last resort, it is the people of South Africa, and they alone, who will have to solve their problem. I firmly believe that we shall.

— Reading No. 30 —

RACE CONFLICT IN SOUTH AFRICA AND THE GENERAL ASSEMBLY OF THE UNITED NATIONS, 1952 [30]

A letter dated September 12, 1952, addressed to the Secretary-General of the United Nations by the permanent representatives of thirteen nations of the Middle East and South Asia, requested that the question of race relations and apartheid be included in the agenda of the seventh regular session of the General Assembly. An explanatory memorandum supported this request.

✓   ✓   ✓

The race conflict in the Union of South Africa resulting from the policies of *apartheid* of the South African Government is creating a dangerous and explosive situation, which constitutes both a threat to international peace and a flagrant violation of the basic principles of human rights and fundamental freedoms which are enshrined in the Charter of the United Nations. . . .

Apartheid, which is the declared objective of the Government of the Union of South Africa, implies a permanent white superiority over the non-Whites, who constitute the great majority of the Union's population. To achieve *apartheid,* the following measures are being taken:

(*a*) Under the notorious Group Areas Act non-Whites are compelled to abandon their present lands and premises and to move to new and usually inferior

[30] *Annex I, Report of the United Nations Commission on the Racial Situation in the Union of South Africa* (New York, 1953) p. 121. Courtesy of the United Nations.

reserved areas without compensation or provisional alternative accommodation;

(b) Complete segregation is enforced in public services, such as railways, buses and post offices;

(c) The Suppression of Communism Act is being used to suppress democratic movements, especially of the non-Whites, for example, those which advocate racial equality or urge opposition to *apartheid;*

(d) Non-Whites are debarred from combat service in the armed forces;

(e) No voting or other political rights whatsoever are enjoyed by non-Whites, except in Cape Province, where Africans and the "Coloured" inhabitants have a limited franchise;

(f) Africans are confined to reserves, and their movements are restricted to certain places after specified hours under certain restrictive laws. The interprovincial movements of non-Whites are also restricted;

(g) Non-Whites are excluded under the Mines Works Amendment Act of 1926 from certain classes of skilled work and a systematic drive is in progress to replace them, even in the lower grades of the public services, by Whites;

(h) The education of non-Whites and their housing and living conditions are deplorable. Such facilities of this type as are available to non-Whites are vastly inferior to those offered to the White population.

As a result of these measures, a social system is being evolved under which the non-Whites, who constitute 80 per cent of the population of the Union of South Africa, will be kept in a permanently inferior state to the White minority. Such a policy challenges all that the United Nations stands for and clearly violates the basic and fundamental objectives of the Charter of the United Nations.

— Reading No. 31 —

THE UNITED NATIONS ANALYZES THE RACIAL SITUATION IN SOUTH AFRICA, 1953 [31]

A United Nations commission was authorized by the General Assembly to investigate the taut and menacing racial situation in the Union of South Africa. While the commission was barred from the Union, it was able to prepare an exhaustive and penetrating report based on a mass of documentary material and testimony from many witnesses.

ⵉ   ⵉ   ⵉ

The members of the Commission are aware that prophecy is within neither their terms of reference nor their capacity. Nevertheless, they believe that it is their duty as free and responsible men to transmit to the Assembly a conviction which they bore in mind during their long work and which was strengthened daily. They wished to communicate their concern to the Assembly. They reached the following conclusions:

(*a*) It is highly unlikely, and indeed improbable, that the policy of *apartheid* will ever be willingly accepted by the masses subjected to discrimination;

(*b*) Efforts at persuasion, however powerful they may be or become, by the Government and Europeans can never convince the non-Europeans that the policy is based on justice and a wish to promote their material and moral interests, and not on pride of race and a will to domination;

(*c*) As the *apartheid* policy develops, the situation it has made is constantly being aggravated and daily be-

[31] *Report of the United Nations Commission on the Racial Situation in the Union of South Africa, General Assembly, Eighth Session* (New York, 1953) pp. 117-119. Courtesy of the United Nations.

comes less open to settlement by conciliation, persuasion, information or education, daily more explosive and menacing to internal peace and to the foreign relations of the Union of South Africa. Soon any solution will be precluded and the only way out will be through violence, with all its inevitable and incalculable dangers. Moreover, in this atmosphere of growing tension there is a danger that the forces of agitation and subversion, which the Government is resisting by strong legislative measures, will find an increasingly favorable soil; there is a serious risk that they may come into the hands of non-Europeans and eventually be regarded by these as a hopeful instrument of liberation.

906. The members of the Commission, faced with a situation which is so serious and which seems to them to be fraught with such grave and imminent threats, feel in duty bound to communicate to the Assembly for its consideration on certain suggestions which have occurred to them concerning the assistance which the community of peoples convened in the United Nations could, and therefore should, give to help a Member, the Union of South Africa, to solve those problems at a difficult moment in its history. The members of the Commission realize that the Commission was set up for inquiry and not as a commission of good offices, but are willing to risk reproach for an unduly wide interpretation of their terms of reference if they make the following suggestions.

907. (i) The competent organs of the United Nations, especially the General Assembly, are the guardians of the principles of the San Francisco Charter. It is their duty to affirm those principles clearly and firmly whenever to do so seems necessary. Human beings in general, and especially those who are persecuted, who suffer injustice . . . have the right to hope that the Organization which was set up at San Francisco under the sign of "faith in fundamental human rights" will be the first to give them its moral support. . . .

908. (ii) Nevertheless, international cooperation has another duty as important if not more important: to face reality and seek by all peaceful means . . . a manner in which to help to solve problems. Every Member State going through a serious and difficult period is entitled

to receive aid and assistance. This aid must include all
the friendly advice which the great family of the United
Nations is able to give to one of its Members in a
spirit of brotherhood. In the case of the Union of South
Africa, there is a great opportunity to give both moral
and material aid and assistance and thus to confirm international solidarity and cooperation by deeds.

The United Nations, in view of its serious anxiety at
the development of ethnic tensions in South Africa and
at the feelings which those tensions have aroused in
other States . . . might *express the hope* that the Government of the Union of South Africa will be able to
reconsider the components of its policy towards various
ethnic groups. The United Nations might *suggest* ways
and means in which the Union might draw up a new
policy; for example, a round table conference of members of different ethnic groups of the Union, which
would . . . make proposals to the Government to
facilitate the peaceful development of the racial situation
in the Union of South Africa. . . .

909. (iii) Nevertheless, the South African racial problem cannot be solved by the mere wish of a government
which has decided to change its policy. . . . The Commission therefore considers that the best course of international cooperation would be to offer the Government
of the Union of South Africa at an opportune moment
all the material and intellectual assistance which an
international organization should and can give to one of
its Members in difficulty. This assistance, if it were requested and accepted, might take the form of carrying
out studies, setting up conciliation machinery, or lending,
through technical, financial, economic and social assistance, the Organization's effective support to a policy and
projects aimed at facilitating, in education, health, housing, agriculture, industry and public works, the maintenance of peaceful relations among the ethnic groups
of the Union of South Africa and the progressive development of their collaboration in the life of the community.

ASPECTS OF COLONIAL POLICY IN THE BELGIAN CONGO, 1954 [32]

Belgian colonial rule stands in a class by itself, different from the British on the one hand and from the French and Portuguese on the other. Like the British, the Belgians show no determination to make the African native into a European counterpart of his ruler; on the other hand, unlike the British, they show little desire to give the Africans training in the institutions of democracy. Unrivaled in any other colonial area in Africa is the degree to which the native Congolese have been trained as skilled artisans and technicians in the factories and the mines.

⁂

Primitive Congolese society consisted of the rulers, the elders of the tribe and the anonymous hoi-polloi. The basic principles of the social and political structure was a kind of paternalism, that all too often degenerated into brutal tyranny. In fact, the people had little voice in their own affairs and the very idea of democracy would have been considered by those in power as an heresy. White paternalism has been decried nearly as much as colonialism itself. It has been represented as an attack on the dignity of man. It certainly is objectionable when one deals with people who socially and intellectually are full grown. It is not when one has to educate to modern ways a population that is supposed to have covered in 50 years the road the western world took more than two thousand years to travel.

The mental inferiority of the Congolese has never been an axiom of Belgian colonial action. On the con-

[32] *Belgian Congo—American Survey* (New York, 1954) pp. 38-44. Courtesy of the Belgian Embassy.

trary, the educators, administrators and missionaries
have always contended that the possibilities of the Congolese were those of any man anywhere else. Consequently, the idea of discrimination and racial superiority
was absent from their policy. However, a *de facto* distinction was made between those Congolese who already
have achieved a degree of civilization, mental as well as
technical, and those who have not yet done so. In western society, we discriminate against people who do not
wash, or whose way of speech is objectionable; we discriminate all the time in order to preserve our civilization . . . and to educate the boor and the country-
bumpkin. That kind of discrimination exists and will
continue to exist until the majority of the Congolese
have attained a certain degree of evolution.

To prepare the way, the Belgians have improved the
housing of the Congolese, they have taught him the
elements of hygiene, they have taught him to dress
decently and practically, they have shown him the advantage of membership in clubs and societies. They have
put into his hands the great means of communication of
our day, the radio, the press, the film. . . . Human contact on the social level between whites and Congolese
remains the cornerstone of a harmonious society. This
is achieved in clubs and circles where both groups mingle and discuss freely and on equal terms. It is also
obtained in the schools where, after careful selection,
both races are admitted without discrimination. . . .

Of all the systems devised by man to regulate his
relationship to the community, democracy . . . has
proved to be the one which guarantees best the dignity
of man. . . . The desire for freedom may be innate in
the human heart, it is practically realized only after a
long struggle and it is a task of everybody to preserve
it. Ancient Congolese society ignored democracy. It was
based on power. The dynastic history of the royal house
of Ruanda-Urundi is a tale of horror. . . . Murder,
poisoning, extreme cruel disfiguration, were the political
weapons. With all that the Belgians have done away.
They respected within certain limits the established order:
the local chiefs are confirmed in their power, as democratic methods could not have been introduced over-
night, but the chiefs are no longer absolute rulers. They

are expected to live up to a code of rulership and as
soon as they transgress it, they are removed and replaced.
This political education does take time, but in recent
years very few of the chiefs had to be removed from
office. . . .

To what extent do the Congolese participate in the
government of their own affairs? This question, often
asked, is as much a leading question as the classic: Have
you stopped beating your wife? Because the premise of
the discussion should be that nobody, white or colored,
has the franchise in the Congo, and that in their present
stage, the majority of the population does not have an
idea what effective government is all about.

To teach the Congolese how a modern government
works, they are introduced progressively into the advisory councils of the Government, they have their
representatives in all the important bodies on an equal
footing with the whites. . . .

Without false modesty, the Belgians can say to the
world, to the ignorant sentimentalists who deplore the
disappearance of the picturesque old ways of primitive
society, as well as to the hypocritical critics who
treat them as exploiters of the natives: "Look at the
Belgian Congo today, look at what we have done in
scarcely half a century, look at the roads, the cities, the
industries, the churches and the schools, above all, look
at the millions of primitive, miserable beings we are
making into citizens of the world."

— Reading No. 33 —

THE FRENCH UNION, 1946[33]

[33] *Constitution of the French Republic* (Paris, 1946). Prepared by the French Embassy, Press and Information
Division, Washington, D.C. Courtesy of the French Embassy.

*Forming part of the constitution of the French Republic,
the French Union provided for the representation of all
departments and territories overseas in bodies functioning in Paris. At the same time representative bodies were
established in the territories to teach and train the people
to manage their own affairs along democratic lines. In
effect, the Union was an attempt to liberalize the empire
by offering self-government to all the parts of an indissoluble unit.*

✔   ✔   ✔

PREAMBLE

France shall form with the people of her Overseas
Territories a Union based upon equality of rights and
privileges, without distinction as to race or religion.

The French Union shall be composed of nations and
peoples who shall place in common or coordinate their
resources and their efforts in order to develop their respective civilizations, further their well-being, and ensure
their security.

Faithful to her traditional mission, France shall guide
the peoples for whom she has assumed responsibility,
toward freedom to govern themselves and toward the
democratic administration of their own affairs; rejecting
any system of colonization based upon arbitrary power,
she shall guarantee to all equal access to public office
and the individual or collective exercise of the rights and
liberties . . . proclaimed or confirmed. . . .

TITLE VIII: THE FRENCH UNION

Section I—Principles

ARTICLE 60. The French Union shall be composed,
on the one hand, of the French Republic which com-
prises Metropolitan France and the Overseas Departments and Territories, and, on the other hand, of the
Associated Territories and States.

ARTICLE 61. The position of the Associated States
within the French Union shall, in the case of each individual State, depend upon the Act that defines its relationship to France.

ARTICLE 62. The members of the French Union shall
place all their resources so as to guarantee the defense

of the whole Union. The Government of the Republic shall coordinate these resources and direct such policies as will prepare and ensure this defense.

Section II—Organization

ARTICLE 63. The central organs of the French Union shall be: the President, the High Council and the Assembly.

ARTICLE 64. The President of the French Republic shall be the President of the French Union; he shall represent its permanent interests.

ARTICLE 65. The High Council of the French Union, under the chairmanship of the President of the Union, shall be composed of a delegation of the French Government and of the representatives that each Associated State shall accredit to the President of the Union.

Its function shall be to assist the Government in the general conduct of the affairs of the Union.

ARTICLE 66. The Assembly of the French Union shall be composed half of members representing Metropolitan France and half of members representing the Overseas Departments and Territories and the Associated States.

An organic law shall determine the mode of representation of the different sections of the population.

ARTICLE 67. The members of the Assembly of the Union shall be elected by the Territorial Assemblies for the Overseas Departments and Territories; for Metropolitan France, two thirds shall be elected by the National Assembly representing Metropolitan France and one third by the Council of the Republic also representing Metropolitan France.

ARTICLE 68. The Associated States may appoint delegates to the Assembly of the French Union within the limitations and conditions determined by a law and by an act individual to each State.

ARTICLE 69. The President of the French Union shall convoke the Assembly of the French Union and shall close its sessions. He must convene it upon the request of half of its members.

The Assembly of the Union may not sit during recesses of Parliament. . . .

ARTICLE 71. The Assembly of the French Union shall examine the bills or proposals submitted to it by the

National Assembly or the Government of the French
Republic or the Governments of the Associated States,
in order that it may give its opinion thereon.

The Assembly shall be empowered to express its opinion on resolutions proposed by one of its members and, if
these resolutions are accepted for deliberation, to instruct
its Secretariat to send them to the National Assembly.
It may submit proposals to the French Government and
to the High Council of the French Union.

In order to be admissible, the proposed resolutions
referred to in the preceding paragraph must concern
legislation pertaining to the Overseas Territories.

ARTICLE 72. Legislative powers with regard to penal
law, civil liberties, and political and administrative
organization in the Overseas Territories, shall rest with
Parliament [that is, the French Legislature].

In all other matters, the French law shall be applicable
in the Overseas Territories only by an express provision
to that effect, or if it has been extended to the Overseas
Territories by decree, after consultation with the Assembly of the Union.

Moreover . . . special provisions for each Territory
may be enacted by the President of the Republic in the
Council of Ministers, after preliminary consultation with
the Assembly of the Union.

Section III—The Overseas Departments and Territories

ARTICLE 73. The legislative regime of the Overseas
Departments shall be the same as that of the Departments of Metropolitan France, save for exceptions determined by law.

ARTICLE 74. The Overseas Territories shall be granted
a special statute which takes into account their particular
interests with relation to the general interests of the
Republic.

This statute and the internal organization of each
Overseas Territory or group of Territories shall be determined by law after the Assembly of the French Union
has expressed its opinion thereon, and after consultation
with the Territorial Assemblies.

ARTICLE 75. The status of the respective members of

the French Republic and of the French Union shall be subject to change.

Modifications of status and passage from one category to another within the framework established in Article 60 may take place only as the result of a law passed by Parliament, after consultation with the Territorial Assemblies and the Assembly of the Union.

ARTICLE 76. The representative of the Government in each Territory or group of Territories shall be vested with the powers of the Republic. He shall be the administrative head of the Territory.

He shall be responsible to the Government for his actions.

ARTICLE 77. An elective Assembly shall be instituted in each Territory. The electoral regime, composition and powers of this Assembly shall be determined by law.

ARTICLE 78. In the groups of territories, the management of matters of common interest shall be entrusted to an Assembly composed of members elected by the Territorial Assemblies.

ARTICLE 79. The Overseas Territories shall elect representatives to the National Assembly and to the Council of the Republic under conditions determined by law.

ARTICLE 80. All subjects of the Overseas Territories shall be citizens with the same status as French nationals of Metropolitan France or of the Overseas Territories. Special laws shall determine the conditions under which they may exercise their rights as citizens.

ARTICLE 81. All French nationals and subjects of the French Union shall have the status of citizens of the French Union, and thereby they shall be ensured the enjoyment of the rights and liberties guaranteed by the Preamble of the present Constitution.

PORTUGAL'S ASSIMILATION POLICY OF NATIVE PEOPLES, 1950 [34]

A Portuguese official attached as an economic expert to the Government General of the Colony of Angola explains the basic philosophy of his country's rule in this African possession.

It is a fact commented upon by everybody that in the Portuguese colonies, whether localized in Africa, Asia or Australasia, a peaceful atmosphere has prevailed now for centuries, in startling contrast to the state of affairs at present observed in the same continents, in territories governed by other nations.

This fact is the outcome of our policy of assimilation of native peoples, markedly realistic and based upon an experience of long centuries of civilizing action, by means of which we are gradually raising them to our level so that in time we will make them all as Portuguese as the Portuguese of the Mother-Country, distinct from these only in their color.

To attain this end, we do not close our eyes to the objective reality which the native problem presents, and therefore do not confuse the civilized and semi-civilized natives living in towns and their outskirts, which constitute a minority, with the vast mass of raw, uneducated natives peopling the remainder of the territory.

In our opinion, to mix up a native of the bush with one that has lived close to us, absorbed our ways, habits and ideals—in a word, our civilization—and to seek to apply to the former the methods of approach

[34] A. J. Alfaro Cardoso, *Angola Your Neighbor* (Johannesburg, 1950) pp. 71-72. Courtesy of the Portuguese Embassy.

that we adopt with the latter, is to run away from the reality of fact, leaving the problem without adequate solution.

The raw native is unacquainted with the most elementary principles of hygiene, whether with regard to his dwelling or his feeding or still the care of his body; he works his lands by using the most primitive implements and processes; he raises his cattle by following the teachings of nature learnt in the observation of the life of wild animals around him; he practices fetish-worship, endowing trees, streams and all inanimate objects with life and believing that they can influence him for good or evil.

This raw native has to be looked at as an adult with a child's mentality—and as such he must be considered. He needs to be tutored as if he were a minor, taught to feed and clothe himself properly and to withstand the dangers that face him on all sides, shown how to get the most out of his own land by the best methods, guided in the choice of work suited to his abilities—in short, educated, physically, morally and professionally.

What he consequently requires is protection and teaching, until he grows up and, as a civilized man, can take his place beside us.

Bearing this in mind, the enlightening action of the Portuguese in Africa has been characteristically "paternal," slowly but surely improving the native's standards of living and bringing him towards our sphere of life and into closer touch with ourselves, so that gradually he will come to adopt our culture, language and faith.

For this purpose our Government and the Missions it subsidizes maintain, throughout the Colony, a large number of schools where Africans learn to speak, read and write our language; [also provided are] experimental farms where they are taught to cultivate their lands and raise their cattle, and work-shop schools where such trades as carpentry, masonry, painting, printing and so on, are instilled into them.

That is the reason why we find to-day, in Angola, a high percentage of natives exercising the most varied professions, such as those given above. They are not only semi-skilled, but skilled artisans of all types. Everywhere in the territory we see them at work, and the fact that they feel equally at home with their white masters is the foundation on which we build our peaceful colonizing policy.

The result of the foregoing is that we do not practise racial discrimination. What we want to see is that the individual, be he white, yellow or black, should possess moral and civic education and culture—should be, in a word, a civilized man.

All those who reach our standards enjoy among us the same rights, and stand in a position of perfect equality with us, irrespective of the colour of their skins.

SELECT BIBLIOGRAPHY

Awolowo, Obafemi, *Path to Nigerian Freedom* (Faber & Faber, Ltd., London, 1947).

Bartlett, Vernon, *Struggle for Africa* (Frederick A. Praeger, New York, 1953).

Batten, T. R., *Problems of African Development* (Oxford University Press, London, 1947).

Bourrett, F. M., *The Gold Coast* (Stanford University Press, Stanford, Calif., 1949).

Brown, William O., ed., "Contemporary Africa: Trends and Issues," *The Annals of the American Academy of Political and Social Science* (Philadelphia, March 1955).

Buell, R. L., *The Native Problem in Africa,* 2 vols. (The Macmillan Co., New York, 1928).

Campbell, Alexander, *The Heart of Africa* (Alfred A. Knopf, Inc., New York, 1954).

Cook, Arthur N., *British Enterprise in Nigeria* (University of Pennsylvania Press, Philadelphia, 1943).

Catroux, General Georges, "The French Union," *International Conciliation* (New York, 1953).

Crocker, W. R., *Self-Government for the Colonies* (George Allen & Unwin, Ltd., London, 1949).

Davidson, Basil, ed., *The New West Africa* (George Allen & Unwin, Ltd., London, 1953).

De Kiewiet, C. W., *A History of South Africa* (Oxford University Press, London, 1941).

Delavignette, Robert, *Freedom and Authority in French West Africa* (Oxford University Press, London, 1950).

Dilley, Marjorie R., *British Policy in Kenya Colony* (Thomas Nelson & Sons, New York, 1937).

Farson, Negley, *Last Chance in Africa* (Harcourt, Brace and Company, Inc., New York, 1950).

Hailey, Lord, *An African Survey* (Oxford University Press, London, 1945).

Haines, C. Grove, *Africa Today* (Johns Hopkins Press, Baltimore, 1955).

Hatch, John, *The Dilemma of South Africa* (Dennis Dobson, Ltd., London, 1952).

Huxley, Elspeth, and Margery Perham, *Race and Politics in Kenya* (Faber & Faber, Ltd., London, 1944).

Huxley, Julian, *Africa View* (Harper & Brothers, New York, 1931).

Keppel-Jones, Arthur, *South Africa* (Hutchinson's University Library, London, n.d.).

Leakey, L. S. B., *Mau Mau and the Kikuyu* (Methuen & Co., Ltd., London, 1952).

Legum, Colin, *Must We Lose Africa?* (W. H. Allen, London, 1954).

Lugard, Sir Frederick D., *The Dual Mandate in British Tropical Africa* (William Blackwood & Sons, Ltd., Edinburgh, 1926).

Marquard, Leo, *The Peoples and Policies of South Africa* (Oxford University Press, London, 1952).

Padmore, George, *The Gold Coast Revolution* (Dennis Dobson, Ltd., London, 1953).

Stamp, L. Dudley, *Africa: A Study in Tropical Development* (John Wiley & Sons, Inc., New York, 1953).

Townsend, Mary E., *The Rise and Fall of Germany's Colonial Empire* (The Macmillan Co., New York, 1930).

Welsh, Anne, ed., *Africa South of the Sahara* (Oxford University Press, London, 1951).

Westermann, Diedrich, *The African Today and To-morrow* (Oxford University Press, London, 1939).

Wieschhoff, H. A., *Colonial Policies in Africa* (University of Pennsylvania Press, Philadelphia, 1944).

Wright, Richard, *Black Power* (Harper & Brothers, New York, 1954).

INDEX

VAN NOSTRAND ANVIL BOOKS already published